ACCA FOUNDATION LEVEL

FAU

Foundations in Audit

EXAM KIT

FAU: FOUNDATIONS IN AUDIT

British Library Cataloguing-in-Publication Data

A catalogue record for this book is available from the British Library.

Published by Kaplan Publishing UK

Unit 2 The Business Centre

Molly Millar's Lane

Wokingham

Berkshire

RG41 2QZ

ISBN: 978-1-78740-343-7

© Kaplan Financial Limited, 2018

Printed and bound in Great Britain.

The text in this material and any others made available by any Kaplan Group company does not amount to advice on a particular matter and should not be taken as such. No reliance should be placed on the content as the basis for any investment or other decision or in connection with any advice given to third parties. Please consult your appropriate professional adviser as necessary. Kaplan Publishing Limited and all other Kaplan group companies expressly disclaim all liability to any person in respect of any losses or other claims, whether direct, indirect, incidental, consequential or otherwise arising in relation to the use of such materials.

All rights reserved. No part of this publication may be reproduced, stored in a retrieval system, or transmitted, in any form or by any means, electronic, mechanical, photocopying, recording or otherwise, without the prior written permission of Kaplan Publishing.

Acknowledgements

The past ACCA exam questions are the copyright of the Association of Chartered Certified Accountants. The original answers to the questions from June 2006 onwards were produced by the examiners themselves and have been adapted by Kaplan Publishing.

We are grateful to the Chartered Institute of Management Accountants and the Institute of Chartered Accountants in England and Wales for permission to reproduce past exam questions. The answers have been prepared by Kaplan Publishing.

These materials are reviewed by the ACCA examining team. The objective of the review is to ensure that the material properly covers the syllabus and study guide outcomes, used by the examining team in setting the exams, in the appropriate breadth and depth. The review does not ensure that every eventuality, combination or application of examinable topics is addressed by the ACCA Approved Content. Nor does the review comprise a detailed technical check of the content as the Approved Content Provider has its own quality assurance processes in place in this respect.

INTRODUCTION

The exam kit for 2018 has been updated and is packed with exam-type questions. This book will help you to successfully prepare for your exam.

- Questions are grouped by syllabus topics and provide extensive coverage of all syllabus areas.
- Many questions are of exam standard and format – this enables you to master the exam techniques.

PAPER ENHANCEMENTS

We have added the following enhancements to the answers in this exam kit:

Key answer tips

Some answers include key answer tips to help your understanding of each question.

Tutorial note

Some answers include tutorial notes to explain some of the technical points in more detail.

CONTENTS

	Page
Index to questions and answers	P.7
Syllabus and revision guidance	P.11
The exam	P.19

Section

1	Multiple-choice questions	1
2	Practice questions	35
3	Answers to multiple-choice questions	81
4	Answers to practice questions	95
5	June 12 Exam questions	175
6	Answers to June 12 Exam questions	181

Quality and accuracy are of the utmost importance to us so if you spot an error in any of our products, please send an email to mykaplanreporting@kaplan.com with full details.

Our Quality Co-ordinator will work with our technical team to verify the error and take action to ensure it is corrected in future editions.

INDEX TO QUESTIONS AND ANSWERS

	Page number
	Question	Answer

MULTIPLE CHOICE QUESTIONS

	Question	Answer
The business environment	1	81
The audit framework	2	81
Audit planning and risk	7	82
Internal control	12	85
Audit evidence (including computer-based systems) and sampling	21	89
Audit completion	30	93

PRACTICE QUESTIONS

THE BUSINESS ENVIRONMENT

		Question	Answer
1	Advantages of audit	35	95
2	X Co	35	96
3	Limitation of liability of auditors	36	97
4	External auditors	37	99
5	External auditor responsibilities	37	99

THE AUDIT FRAMEWORK

		Question	Answer
6	Eagle Co	37	100
7	Sparrow Co	37	100
8	Ethics	38	101
9	Fastbikes	38	102
10	Sujon	39	102
11	Responsibilities regarding fraud	39	103
12	Audit programmes	39	103
13	Independence problems	39	104
14	Viswa	40	105
15	Audit working papers	40	106
16	P and Partners	40	107

AUDIT PLANNING AND RISK

		Question	Answer
17	Finch Co	41	107
18	Williams	42	109
19	Jip	43	110
20	Arnold	43	111
21	Wizzin	44	112
22	Yes Houses	44	112

FAU: FOUNDATIONS IN AUDIT

		Page number	
		Question	*Answer*
23	Materiality	45	113
24	Tightrope	45	113
25	Audit risk	46	115
26	Brahms Co	46	116
27	Mozart Co	46	117
28	Tulip Co	47	117
29	Parker	47	119

ACCOUNTING SYSTEMS AND CONTROLS (INCLUDING COMPUTER-BASED SYSTEMS)

General principles

30	DS	48	120
31	Woods	49	121
32	Forest	49	121
33	Show	49	122
34	Doors	50	123
35	Rose Co	50	125

Ascertaining and recording the system

36	Hocatta	51	127

Revenue and receivables

37	Car parking	52	128
38	Green	53	128
39	Londglas & Co	53	129
40	Haydn Co	54	130

Inventory and purchasing

41	Starling	55	133
42	Smartbuy	55	134
43	M	56	135
44	Zed	56	135

Payroll

45	Peach Co	57	135
46	Cafés	58	138
47	Recruitment	59	139

Management letter

48	Lake Foundry	60	139
49	Ventair	61	141

Evaluation techniques and testing

50	Shirts	62	143

INDEX TO QUESTIONS AND ANSWERS

		Page number	
		Question	*Answer*

Controls in computer systems

51	Kola	62	144
52	Oilco	63	145
53	Sometech	64	146
54	Semi	64	146
55	Fozz	65	147

AUDIT EVIDENCE (INCLUDING COMPUTER-BASED SYSTEMS) AND SAMPLING

General principles

56	Audit evidence I	65	148
57	Audit evidence II	66	150
58	Audit evidence III	66	151
59	Audit evidence IV	67	151
60	Employment as a junior auditor	67	152

Inventory

61	Diamond	67	152
62	Emerald	68	153
63	Coaches	68	153
64	Sweet Scents	69	154
65	Jeans	69	155

Non-current assets

66	Andrew Manufacturing	70	156

Receivables

67	Askwith	71	159

Cash

68	Bon Voyage	72	160

Liabilities and other items

69	Pear Co	73	161
70	Apple Co	73	161
71	Farrington	73	162
72	Oxton Wholesalers	74	162
73	Clothing	74	163

Sampling

74	Audit sampling	75	163
75	Cromwell	75	163

KAPLAN PUBLISHING

FAU: FOUNDATIONS IN AUDIT

		Page number	
		Question	*Answer*

AUDIT COMPLETION

76	Review and reporting	76	164
77	Auditors' opinion	76	165
78	Going concern	76	165
79	Toby	76	166
80	Going concern concept	77	166
81	Lambley Properties	77	167

AUDIT REPORT

82	Jones, Roberts, Williams	78	168
83	Taggart	79	170
84	B Co	70	171
85	Gee	80	172
86	Butcar and Company	80	172
87	Types of audit opinion	80	174

SYLLABUS AND REVISION GUIDANCE

SYLLABUS CONTENT

The FAU paper requires knowledge and understanding of FAB (Accountant in Business), FMA (Management Accounting) and FFA (Financial Accounting).

SYLLABUS

A   BUSINESS ENVIRONMENT AND AUDIT FRAMEWORK (Chapters 1, 2, 3, 4, 5, 19)

(1) The purpose and scope of an audit

(2) The legal duties of auditors

(3) Professional ethics and the ACCA Code of Ethics

(4) Auditor engagement and liability

(5) Audit regulation

(6) Internal audit

B   AUDIT PLANNING AND RISK (Chapter 6)

(1) Audit risk

(2) Understanding the entity and its environment

(3) Audit strategy and the audit plan

(4) Audit documentation

C   INTERNAL CONTROL (Chapters 7, 8)

(1) General principles of internal control

(2) Techniques to understand, record and evaluate accounting systems

(3) Tests of controls

(4) Communication on internal control

D   AUDIT EVIDENCE AND PROCEDURES (Chapters 9 – 15)

(1) Audit evidence and assertions

(2) Audit procedures

(3) Substantive procedures

(4) Audit sampling

(5) Computer-assisted audit techniques (CAATs)

E   AUDIT COMPLETION (Chapters 16, 17)

    (1)   Going concern

    (2)   Subsequent events

    (3)   Written representations

    (4)   Auditor's Report

Excluded topics

The following topics are specifically excluded from the syllabus:

- group audits
- corporate governance
- detailed understanding of audit requirements relating to:
    - fraud
    - auditing standards on laws and regulations
    - related parties
    - service organisations
    - reporting to regulators in the financial sector.

Key areas of the syllabus

The key topic areas are as follows:

- audit planning
- practical application of audit techniques
- preparing draft reports.

STUDY GUIDE

A   BUSINESS ENVIRONMENT AND AUDIT FRAMEWORK

1   The purpose and scope of an audit

    (a)   Explain the nature of an audit.

    (b)   Explain the purpose of an audit, including the advantages and disadvantages of an audit.

    (c)   Explain the nature of accounting records, including proper records.

    (d)   Explain the concept of true and fair presentation, and reasonable assurance.

    (e)   Identify the form and content of the auditors' report.

2   The legal duties of auditors

    (a)   Describe the duties of auditors.

    (b)   Describe the rights of auditors.

3 Professional ethics

(a) Discuss the fundamental principles of professional ethics of integrity, objectivity, professional competence and due care, confidentiality, and professional behaviour

(b) Describe the detailed requirements, and application of professional ethics, in the context of integrity, objectivity and independence

(c) Describe the auditor's responsibility with regard to confidentiality

4 Auditor engagement and liability

(a) Explain the factors that auditors should consider before accepting an audit engagement

(b) Explain the purpose and nature of an engagement letter

(c) Explain the liability of auditors under contract and negligence to clients.

(d) Explain the liability of auditors to third parties.

5 Audit regulation

(a) Explain the scope of ISAs.

6 Internal audit

(a) Explain the purpose and scope of an internal audit function

(b) Identify the factors that external auditors should consider when evaluating the work of internal auditors.

B AUDIT PLANNING AND RISK ASSESSMENT

1 Audit risk

(a) Define audit risk, including inherent risk, control risk and detection risk.

(b) Explain the risk-based approach to the audit

(c) Define the concept of materiality.

2 Understanding the entity and its environment

(a) Explain how auditors obtain an initial understanding of the entity and its environment.

3 Audit strategy and the audit plan

(a) Identify and explain the need for planning an audit.

(b) Identify and describe the contents of the overall audit strategy and the audit plan.

(c) Explain the use of analytical procedures in planning.

(d) Describe general planning issues including the availability and management of audit resources, the effect of information technology on audit procedure, the audit of complex areas and the need to use experts

(e) Explain the role of audit programmes and the advantages and disadvantages of using standard audit programmes.

FAU: FOUNDATIONS IN AUDIT

4   Audit documentation

(a) Describe the reasons for maintaining audit documentation.

(b) Explain the purpose and contents of the current file and the permanent file.

(c) Explain the quality control procedures that should exist over the review of audit working papers.

(d) Explain how information technology (IT) may be used in the documentation of audit work.

C   INTERNAL CONTROL

1   General principles of internal control

(a) Describe the five components of an internal control system.

(b) Describe the objectives of an internal control system.

(c) Describe the inherent limitations of an internal control system.

(d) Explain the importance of internal control to auditors.

2   Techniques to understand, record and evaluate accounting systems

(a) Describe the techniques used by auditors to understand and record accounting systems including narrative notes and flowcharts.

(b) Describe the techniques used by auditors to evaluate accounting systems including internal control questionnaires (ICQs), internal control evaluation questionnaires (ICEQs) and checklists.

(c) Provide examples of, and explain the format and contents, ICQs and ICEQs.

(d) Evaluate the internal control system.

3   Tests of controls

(a) Describe and provide examples of control procedures to meet specified objectives for each of the following areas
- purchases and trade payables
- sales and trade receivables
- wages and salaries (payroll)
- tangible non-current assets
- inventory.

(b) Explain the purpose of tests of controls.

(c) Identify and explain the testing of controls over the following areas:
- purchases and trade payables
- sales and trade receivables
- wages and salaries (payroll)
- tangible non-current assets
- inventory.

(d) Distinguish between tests of controls and substantive procedures.

(e) Distinguish between application controls and general IT controls and identify the objectives of each control type.

(f) Provide examples of specific application controls and general IT controls.

SYLLABUS AND REVISION GUIDANCE

4 Communicating control deficiencies

(a) Identify and define significant internal control deficiencies and explain the requirements and methods for communicating significant deficiencies to management and those charged with governance.

D AUDIT EVIDENCE AND PROCEDURES

1 Audit evidence

(a) Explain the importance of audit evidence, including sufficient appropriate audit evidence.

(b) Identify the factors that influence the relevance and reliability of audit evidence.

2 Audit procedures

(a) Explain the importance of the use of the assertions by the auditor.

(b) Explain the assertions in relation to classes of transactions and related disclosures and, account balances and related disclosures.

(c) Describe and give examples of procedures used by auditors to obtain audit evidence, including inspection, observation, external confirmation, recalculation, reperformance, analytical procedures and inquiry

3 Substantive procedures

(a) Explain the rationale for designing audit programmes by reference to audit objectives.

(b) Identify and explain the substantive procedures used in auditing each of the following:

- tangible non-current assets
- investments
- trade receivables, prepayments and other receivables
- trade payables, accruals and other payables
- bank and cash
- non-current liabilities
- provisions.

(c) Explain why the audit of inventory is often an area of high inherent risk.

(d) Describe the audit procedures that should be undertaken before, during and after attending an inventory count.

(e) Describe the extent to which an auditor may rely on a system of perpetual inventory.

(f) Explain the substantive procedures to meet the specific objectives for the audit of inventory.

4 Audit sampling

(a) Define audit sampling and the relevance of sampling to the auditor.

(b) Identify sampling selection methods, including random selection, systematic selection and haphazard selection.

(c) State the main factors affecting sample sizes

5 Computer-assisted audit techniques (CAATs)

(a) Explain the use of CAATs in an audit including the use of audit software and test data.

(b) Explain the advantages and disadvantages of the use of CAATs to the auditor.

E AUDIT COMPLETION

1 Going concern

(a) Define and discuss the significance of going concern.

(b) Discuss indicators of going concern problems.

(c) Explain the procedures to be applied in performing going concern reviews.

2 Subsequent events

(a) Explain the responsibilities of the auditor regarding subsequent events occurring up to the date of the auditor's report.

(b) Explain the procedures to be applied in performing subsequent event reviews.

3 Written representations

(a) Explain the purpose of written representations.

(b) Describe the circumstances where written representations are necessary.

4 Auditor's reports

(a) Describe the form and content of unmodified auditor's reports.

(b) Describe the circumstances, including those where there are identified uncorrected misstatements, in which an auditor should issue a modified auditor's report.

PLANNING YOUR REVISION

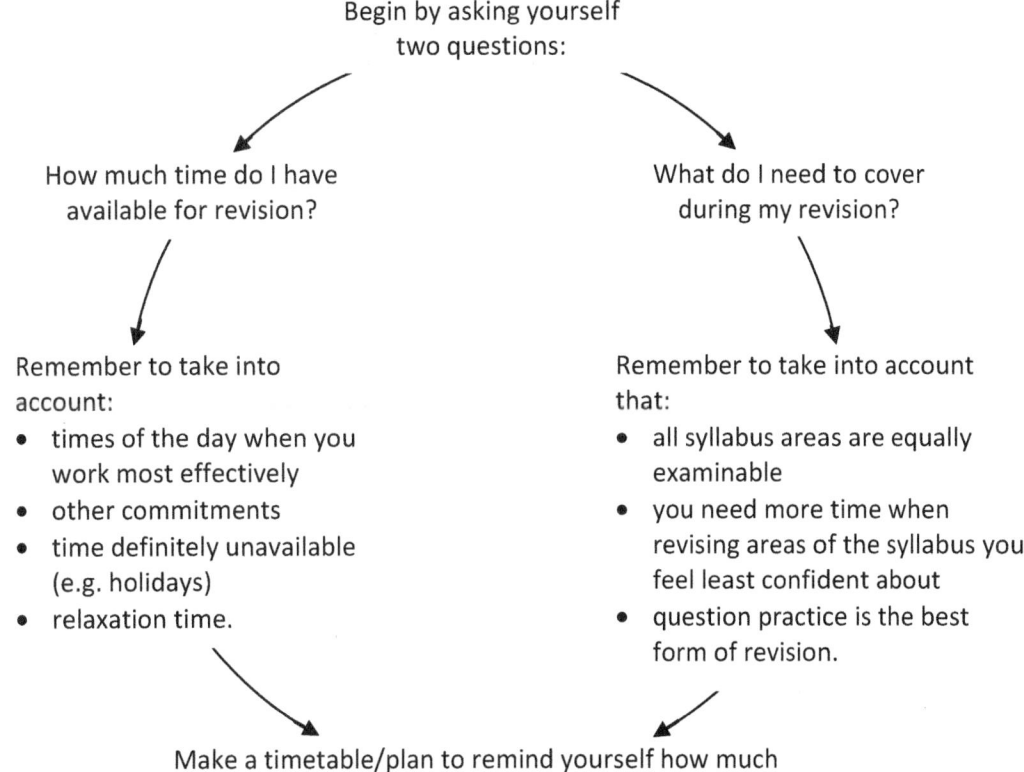

REVISION TECHNIQUES

- Go through your notes and textbook **highlighting the important points**
- You might want to produce your own set of **summarised notes**
- **List key words** for each topic to remind you of the essential concepts
- **Practise exam-standard questions**, under timed conditions
- **Rework questions** that you got completely wrong the first time, but only when you think you know the subject better
- If you get stuck on topics, **find someone to explain** them to you (your tutor or a colleague, for example)
- **Read recent articles** on the ACCA website or in the student magazine
- **Read** good newspapers and professional journals

THE EXAM

FORMAT OF THE EXAMINATION

	Number of marks
Section A	
10 compulsory multiple choice questions of 1, 2 and 3 marks	20
Section B	
Nine compulsory questions	
Q1+2 (15 marks each)	30
Q3+4 (10 marks each)	20
Q5–9 (6 marks each)	30
Total	**100**

Total time allowed: 2 hours

Sitting the examination

Section A questions:

Read each question *very* **carefully.**

Double check your answer before committing yourself to it.

Answer **every** question – if you do not know an answer, you don't lose anything by guessing. Think carefully before you **guess**. The examiner has indicated that many candidates are still leaving blank answers in the real exam.

If you are answering a multiple-choice question, **eliminate first those answers that you know are wrong**. Then choose the most appropriate answer from those that are left.

Section B questions:

Unless you know exactly how to answer the questions, spend some time **planning your answer**. Stick to the question and tailor your answer to what you are asked.

Fully explain all your points.

If you get stuck with a question, return to it later.

Answering the questions

Section B questions: Make a quick plan and under each main point list all the relevant facts you can think of. Then write out your answer developing each point fully. Your text should have a clear structure; it should contain a brief introduction, a main section and a conclusion, where relevant.

Section 1

MULTIPLE-CHOICE QUESTIONS

THE BUSINESS ENVIRONMENT

1   Which of the following is not an objective of external audit?

   A   To enable the auditor to given an opinion on whether the financial statements give a true and fair view of the financial position and performance of the company.

   B   To enable the auditor to given an opinion on whether the financial statements are presented fairly in all material aspects.

   C   To enable the auditor to give an opinion on whether the financial statements are prepared in all material respects, in accordance with an applicable financial reporting framework.

   D   To enable the auditor to give an opinion on whether the financial statements are prepared in all material or immaterial respects, in accordance with an applicable financial reporting framework.

2   Which of the following statements are incorrect regarding external audit?

   1   All companies are required by law to have their annual financial statements audited by an external auditor.

   2   Some organisations like small private companies and partnerships may choose to be audited even if there is no legal requirement.

   3   The financial reporting framework to be applied for external audit varies from country to country.

   4   The external auditor reports on whether the published financial statements are correct or not.

   A   1 and 4
   B   2 and 3
   C   3 and 4
   D   1 and 3

FAU: FOUNDATIONS IN AUDIT

THE AUDIT FRAMEWORK

3   If you are deciding whether a particular accounting policy produces figures that give a true and fair view, which of the following sources of information might you compare the policy with?

   1   Relevant accounting standards (e.g. IAS® Standards and IFRS® Standards).

   2   The accounting standards of specific countries (e.g. US standards or UK standards) if there is no international standard that deals with the topic.

   3   Relevant company law.

   4   The accounting policy used in previous years (if the audit report last year thought that the policy gave a true and fair view, then it probably still does).

   A   1 only

   B   2 and 3 only

   C   1, 2 and 3 only

   D   1, 2, 3 and 4

4   Which of the following may not act as an external auditor?

   1   The members of a professional body authorised by the state.

   2   Those who are unable to comply with ethics rules with respect to independence, objectivity and competence to act as auditor for any particular client.

   3   Those who are prohibited by law from acting as auditor for particular clients.

   A   1 only

   B   2 only

   C   2 and 3 only

   D   1, 2 and 3

5   Which of the following are external auditors NOT responsible for?

   1   Preparing the financial statements.

   2   Choosing accounting policies.

   3   Implementing systems and controls.

   4   Establishing the mechanisms for ensuring that good standards of corporate governance are maintained.

   A   1 and 2

   B   2 and 3

   C   3 and 4

   D   1, 2, 3 and 4

MULTIPLE-CHOICE QUESTIONS : SECTION 1

6 Which of the following applies to the statements below?

1 Error – 'an intentional act involving the use of deception to obtain an unjust or illegal advantage'.

2 Fraud – 'an unintentional mistake' and could include accidental misapplication of accounting policies, oversights or misinterpretation of the facts.

A Statement 1 is true and 2 is false

B Statement 1 is false and 2 is true

C Both statements are true

D Both statements are false

7 Which of the following is true?

A The external auditors are primarily responsible for the prevention and detection of fraud

B The external auditors are responsible for implementing an effective system of internal control

C The directors are responsible for giving an opinion on whether the financial statements are true and fair

D The directors are responsible for safeguarding the company's assets

8 Which of the following is NOT a fundamental principle of professional ethics for an auditor?

A Integrity

B Fraud prevention

C Objectivity

D Professional competence and due care

9 Which fundamental principle of ethics is being breached in the following situation?

You find out that one of your listed audit clients is shortly to be taken over, or has access to technological advances which will give it a fantastic competitive advantage. You decide to buy some shares of the client.

A Integrity

B Due care

C Competence

D Objectivity

10 You have received the latest financial statements, management accounts and supporting documentation for a prospective new client.

What sort of information would NOT lead you to consider this a higher risk assignment than average?

- A Involved in risky/complex business
- B Incompetent/poorly trained staff
- C Business operating from a single location
- D Loss of important staff member/s during the year

11 Which of the following is an example of integrity?

- A Charging the client a lower audit fee than quoted because the work performed took half as long as anticipated.
- B Upon becoming aware of fraudulent activity at the client, not taking steps to prevent further losses as intimidation threats are being made.
- C Taking advantage of a client's poor controls over inventory by helping yourself to a few small immaterial items.
- D Accepting the use of the client's holiday resort for one month because it was graciously offered.

12 Which of the following are independence issues?

1. Working as an audit junior on the statutory audit of a major bank with whom you have your mortgage.
2. Taking on a large new client whose fees will make up 30% of your total revenue
3. Taking on a large new client whose fees will make up 10% of your total revenue.
4. Working as an audit partner and accepting a gold Rolex as a 'gift'.

- A 1 and 3
- B 2 and 4
- C 1 and 2
- D 3 and 4

13 Which of the following is the most appropriate safeguard for the threat given below?

Threat: Auditor provides other services to the client (e.g. accountancy work, tax advice).

- A The auditor refuses one of the engagements
- B Two completely independent teams should be used with different engagement partners
- C Two independent teams should be used with the same engagement partner
- D None of the above

14 Which of the following statements is true regarding confidentiality?

- A Client information must NEVER be disclosed
- B Client information must ALWAYS be disclosed to the tax authorities if so requested
- C If the client gives permission, then disclosure is allowed
- D It is acceptable to leave audit files in cars or in unsecured private residences

15 Which of the following statements is false regarding confidentiality?

- A Disclosure of confidential client information can be made if it is required by law
- B Disclosure of confidential client information can be made if it is in the public interest
- C Disclosure of confidential client information can be made if there is suspicion of terrorism, treason or money laundering
- D Disclosure of confidential client information can be made by the outgoing auditor to the new auditor regardless of whether the client has given permission or not

16 Which of the following is NOT a statutory right of the auditors of a limited company?

1. A right to attend all directors' meetings and receive all noticed and communications relating to such meetings.
2. A right to speak at general meetings on any part of the business that concerns them as auditors.
3. A right to attend any general meeting and receive all notices and communications relating to such meetings.

- A 1 only
- B 1 and 3
- C 2 only
- D 2 and 3

17 Which of the following is incorrect regarding fraud?

- A Auditors can increase the likelihood of detecting fraud by approaching their work with professional scepticism.
- B Auditors should clarify to the client that the responsibility of detecting fraud lies with the auditor whereas that for preventing fraud lies with the client.
- C Auditors should understand their clients, to appreciate how fraud could occur.
- D Auditors should be aware of pressures on directors and management (both personal and business).

18 Which of the following is the most appropriate definition of negligence when considering auditor's liability?

- A Negligence is the deliberate act to cover up deficiencies identified throughout the course of the audit.
- B Negligence is some act or omission which occurs because the person concerned has failed to exercise the degree of care and skill appropriate to the circumstances.
- C Negligence is some act or omission which occurs because the person concerned miscalculated the time necessary to undertake the audit.
- D Negligence is some act or omission which occurs because the person concerned is not yet a qualified accountant.

19 Which of the following assignments could an internal audit department be asked to perform by management?

- A Undertake 'mystery shopper' reviews, where they enter the store as a customer, purchase goods and rate the overall shopping experience.
- B Assist the external auditors by requesting bank confirmation letters.
- C Provide advice on the implementation of a new payroll package for the payroll department.
- D Review the company's financial statements on behalf of the board.

20 A company's internal audit department is going to assist with the statutory audit. The chief internal auditor will provide documentation to the external auditors on the computerised inventory system at the company.

Which of the following matters should the audit team consider in determining whether or not the internal auditor's documentation is adequate for the purposes of the audit?

1 Whether the work was properly planned, performed, supervised, reviewed and documented.

2 Whether sufficient appropriate evidence was obtained to allow the internal auditors to draw reasonable conclusions.

3 Whether the conclusions reached are appropriate in the circumstances and the reports prepared are consistent with the results of the work done.

- A 1 only
- B 1 and 3
- C 2 and 3
- D 1, 2 and 3

AUDIT PLANNING AND RISK

21 Which of the following is NOT true regarding items which are material by nature?

- A An amount may be material by nature because it triggers a threshold
- B An amount may be material by nature because it is a big amount of money
- C An amount may be material by nature because it indicates future developments or other significant events
- D An amount may be material by nature because its disclosure is compulsory

22 Which of the following is an issue which does NOT need to be considered as a part of the planning process of an audit?

- A Problem areas – What issues are likely to cause difficulties and how should they be addressed?
- B Nature of work – What audit approach should be used and what types of procedures are appropriate?
- C Audit opinion – What is the most likely audit opinion to be given at the end of the audit?
- D Amount of work – Sample sizes, number of tests etc. all driven by assessment of risk and materiality.

23 Which of the following are sources of information which enable the auditor to assess risk at the planning stage?

1. Knowledge of the business
2. Analytical review
3. Detailed testing

- A 1 and 2
- B 2 and 3
- C 1 and 3
- D 1, 2 and 3

24 What is the difference between audit strategy and audit plan?

- A Audit strategy sets the overall approach to the audit; the plan fills in the operational details of how the strategy is to be achieved.
- B Audit plan sets the overall approach to the audit; the strategy fills in the operational details of how the plan is to be achieved.
- C Audit strategy details the tests to be conducted whereas audit plan carries out the risk assessment.
- D There is no difference between audit strategy and audit plan.

FAU: FOUNDATIONS IN AUDIT

25 Which of the following is a possible source of knowledge of the business that is to be audited?

1 Last year's audit team.

2 Trade press.

3 Discussions with client staff.

4 Observation of events and processes at the client's premises.

A 1, 2 and 4

B 1, 3 and 4

C 2, 3 and 4

D 1, 2, 3 and 4

26 Audit risk represents the risk that the auditor will give an inappropriate opinion on the financial statements when the financial statements are materially misstated. Which of the following categories of risk can be controlled by the auditor?

1 Control risk.

2 Detection risk.

3 Inherent risk.

A 1 and 2

B 2 only

C 1 and 3

D 2 and 3

27 Which of the following are inherent risks?

1 A client with poor trading results and in danger of breaching its borrowing facilities.

2 Password system is ineffective because everyone knows everyone else's password.

3 Valuable assets not kept in safes or under lock and key.

4 No security system for access to sensitive areas.

5 A client in a volatile industry.

6 Computer systems can be changed or modified without suitable authorisation.

7 High value sales can be made to new customers without checking their credit status, or to existing customers who are over their credit limits the person.

8 The sample picked for testing an account balance is not representative of the population.

9 The auditor has used inappropriate procedures.

A 2, 3, 4, 6 and 7

B 1 and 5

C 8 and 9

D All of them

Note: this question is longer and more detailed than you are likely to experience in the exam, but is a good question to aid revision.

28 Which is the following is true regarding audit risk?

   1   Audit risk is made up of inherent and detection risk.
   2   Detection risk includes sampling risk.
   3   The auditor can minimise detection risk by increasing the sample size.

   A   1 only
   B   2 and 3 only
   C   1 and 3 only
   D   1, 2 and 3

29 Over which component of the audit risk model does the auditor have control?

   A   Inherent risk
   B   Control risk
   C   Detection risk
   D   All of the above

30 Which audit procedure is being defined below?

   'The evaluation of financial information made by a study of the plausible relationships among both financial and non-financial data…..the investigation of identified fluctuations and relationships that are inconsistent with other relevant information or deviate significantly from predicted amounts'.

   A   Analytical procedures
   B   Cut-off testing
   C   Substantive procedures
   D   Directional testing

31 Which of the following can be considered the key components of an audit strategy?

   1   Risk and materiality.
   2   Nature, extent and timing of audit procedures.
   3   Understanding the entity's accounting system and internal controls.

   A   1 and 2 only
   B   1 and 3 only
   C   2 and 3 only
   D   1, 2 and 3

32 Which of the following cannot be considered a limitation of analytical procedures?

- A They require sound knowledge and experience of the entity which may be limited in the first year
- B A high level of expertise is required to interpret the results
- C The reliability of the results depends upon reliability of source data
- D It uses a broad range of data, financial as well as non-financial

33 Which of the following cannot be considered an external source of information for an audit client?

- A Industry publications
- B Lawyers
- C Banks/brokers
- D Previous year's working papers

34 Which of the following statements is incorrect regarding audit risk?

- A High inherent risk means that the risk of material errors arising is high
- B High control risk means that the client's internal controls system is likely to fail to prevent/detect and correct material errors
- C High detection risk means that there is a high risk that substantive procedures will not detect a material misstatement
- D The auditor can minimise audit risk by controlling the inherent and control risks

35 An expert is defined as 'a person or firm possessing special skill, knowledge and experience in a particular field other than accounting and audit'.

Which of the following are likely to be the factors considered if an expert is to be used?

1. The expert's competence.
2. The expert's objectivity.
3. Availability of other evidence regarding the area for which an expert is being used.

- A 1 and 2 only
- B 1 and 3 only
- C 2 and 3 only
- D 1, 2 and 3

36 Which of the following provides a definition of inherent risk?

- A The risk that audit procedures do not detect a material misstatement in an account balance or class of transactions
- B The susceptibility of an account balance or class of transactions to material misstatement, irrespective of related internal controls
- C The risk that a material misstatement could occur which would not be prevented, detected and corrected by the accounting or internal control systems of the client
- D The risk that the financial statements may contain a material misstatement

37 Which of the following provides a definition of control risk?

- A The risk that audit procedures do not detect a material misstatement in an account balance or class of transactions
- B The susceptibility of an account balance or class of transactions to material misstatement, irrespective of related internal controls
- C The risk that a material misstatement could occur which would not be prevented, detected and corrected by the accounting or internal control systems of the client
- D The risk that the financial statements may contain a material misstatement

38 Which of the following provides a definition of detection risk?

- A The risk that audit procedures do not detect a material misstatement in an account balance or class of transactions
- B The susceptibility of an account balance or class of transactions to material misstatement, irrespective of related internal controls
- C The risk that a material misstatement could occur which would not be prevented, detected and corrected by the accounting or internal control systems of the client
- D The risk that the financial statements may contain a material misstatement

39 Are the following statements true or false?

1 All working papers must be held as a hard copy, paper file.
2 Working papers should be sufficiently detailed to support any conclusions made.

- A 1 is true and 2 is false
- B 2 is true and 1 is false
- C Both statements are true
- D Both statements are false

40 Are the following statements true or false?

1 Working papers must record every detail of an assignment.
2 The form and content of working papers is the same for every assignment.

- A 1 is true and 2 is false
- B 2 is true and 1 is false
- C Both statements are true
- D Both statements are false

41 Which of the following would normally be retained on the permanent file maintained for a limited company audit client?

- A Completed checklist of statutory disclosure provision.
- B Extracts of minutes of meetings of the directors.
- C Written representations from management.
- D Copy of the company's legal constitution.

FAU: FOUNDATIONS IN AUDIT

42 Which of the following should be facilitated by the standardisation of substantive procedure working papers?

1 Meeting of specified objectives.

2 Communicating with the staff of the audit client.

3 Delegation of audit work.

A 1 only

B 1 and 3

C 2 and 3

D 3 only

INTERNAL CONTROL

43 Which of the following is an example of 'arithmetic and accounting' as a control?

A Lines of authority defined within an organisation

B Use of reconciliation procedures

C Recruiting the right people for the right job

D Cash being received and recorded by two different people

44 Which of the following is an example of 'segregation of duties' as a control?

A Lines of authority defined within an organisation

B Use of reconciliation procedures

C Recruiting the right people for the right job

D Cash being received and recorded by two different people

45 Which of the following applies to controls in an IT system?

1 Computer-based controls are normally divided into two categories, application controls and general controls.

2 Application controls are controls which are built into the system.

3 General IT controls are policies and procedures that relate to many applications and support the effective functioning of application controls by helping to ensure the continued proper operation of information systems.

4 Range check is an example of a general control.

A All statements are true except for 4

B All statements are false except for 3

C All statements are false except for 2

D All statements are true except for 1

MULTIPLE-CHOICE QUESTIONS : SECTION 1

46 Which of the following is a false statement regarding test of controls?

A With a test of controls, the auditor is interested in whether a control has operated correctly – the size of the transaction is irrelevant.

B With a test of controls, the auditor is interested in whether a control has operated correctly and the size of the transaction is also taken into account.

C The greater the assurance from controls, the less the assurance required from substantive procedures, so the less the level of testing.

D In test of controls, the auditor is checking that the company has been trying to ensure that its financial statements are accurate.

47 In order to conduct tests of controls, the auditor needs to understand the client's systems first. Which of the following tests help the auditor in getting information about the systems?

A Cut-off tests

B Substantive tests

C Walkthrough tests

D Directional tests

48 Which of the following are possible ways of documenting the systems and controls operational at a client?

1 Narrative notes

2 Flow charts

3 Audit programmes

4 Organisational charts

A 1, 2 and 3

B 1, 3, and 4

C 2, 3 and 4

D 1, 2, and 4

49 Control checklists are often used to document systems and controls at a client.

Are the following statements true or false?

1 An Internal Control Questionnaire (ICQ) is a list of all possible controls for each area of the financial statements.

2 Internal Control Evaluation (ICE) questionnaire does not attempt to record ALL controls like an ICQ.

3 For each control objective, an ICE asks for the controls which achieve that objective.

A Statement 1 is true and 2 and 3 are false

B All 3 statements are true

C All 3 statements are false

D Statement 1 and 2 are true and 3 is false

KAPLAN PUBLISHING

50 Which of the following is NOT a limitation of internal controls?

 A Human error in the use of judgement

 B No documentation of the systems done by the client

 C Collusion of staff in circumventing controls

 D Responsible people abusing that responsibility to override controls

51 Each major accounting system should have control objectives and control procedures. The auditor can then perform tests of control to ensure the controls are working.

Which of the following definitions is incorrect?

 A Control objectives – the objectives that the internal controls are seeking to achieve

 B Control procedures – the procedures that should be in place to ensure that the control objectives are achieved

 C Tests of control – audit work performed to generate evidence as to whether the individual account balances are materially misstated or not

 D Internal control – a process for assuring achievement of an organisation's objectives in operational effectiveness and efficiency, reliable financial reporting, and compliance with laws, regulations and policies

52 Which of the following is NOT a control objective in the sales cycle?

 A Sales are made to valid customers

 B Sales are made monthly

 C All sales are recorded accurately

 D Cash is collected within a reasonable period

53 State whether each of the following would be a question from an ICQ or ICE.

 1 Are all new customers credit-checked before goods are sent on credit?

 2 Are all sales orders received in writing on standard, pre-numbered forms?

 A Question 1 is from and ICQ and 2 from ICE

 B Question 1 is from ICE and 2 from ICQ

 C Both questions are from ICQ

 D Both questions are from ICE

54 Which of the following is NOT an objective of controls on the purchase cycle?

 A Goods/services delivered are what were ordered

 B Liabilities are recorded completely and accurately

 C Only valid liabilities are paid and payment is made in a sensible, commercial timescale

 D Payment is made through cheques only

MULTIPLE-CHOICE QUESTIONS : SECTION 1

55 The objectives of controls for the payroll cycle are to ensure that the company will:

    A   pay the right people

    B   pay at the right rate for valid work done.

    C   deal correctly with taxes and other deductions

    D   achieve all of the above

56 State whether each of the following would be a question from an ICQ or ICE.

    Q1   Are all leavers required to provide a resignation letter (or fill in a leavers form) that is dated and signed?

    Q2   Is the monthly pay list reviewed by department heads to ensure that leavers are removed?

    Q3   Could the company pay employees who have left? (Important to auditors as it may indicate fraud).

    A   Q1 is from ICQ and 2 and 3 from ICE

    B   Q1 and 2 are from ICQ and 3 from ICE

    C   Q2 and 3 are from ICQ and 1 from ICE

    D   All 3 questions are from ICQ

57 The external auditor is not responsible for implementing or maintaining internal controls.

Which of the following statements describe what the external auditor needs to do?

    1   Assess internal controls as a source of assurance.

    2   Report material deficiencies in internal controls to those charged with governance.

    3   Participate in management decision making to ensure that the internal controls prevent and detect fraud and misstatements.

    A   1 only

    B   1 and 2 only

    C   1 and 3 only

    D   2 and 3 only

58 Which report is used to report all the deficiencies identified in controls to those charged with governance?

    A   Audit report

    B   Audit programmes

    C   Planning memorandum

    D   Management letter

FAU: FOUNDATIONS IN AUDIT

59 Which of the following controls cannot minimise the risk of non-payment by customers?

- A Quality checks on goods before they are dispatched to the customers
- B Credit limits set for all customers
- C Regular review of balances against credit limits to ensure not breached
- D Reducing/altering payment terms for poor payers

60 Which of the following may be a suitable explanation for the term 'control environment'?

1. It includes governance and management function.
2. It includes the attitudes, awareness and actions of those charged with governance.
3. It takes into account the importance of internal controls for the management.

- A 1 and 2 only
- B 1 and 3 only
- C 2 and 3 only
- D 1, 2 and 3

61 Are either/both of the following two statements true or false?

1. Risks and controls for the revenue system are the same in every company.
2. If all customers pay cash up front, the risk of payment default is low.

- A 1 is true and 2 is false
- B 2 is true and 1 is false
- C Both statements are true
- D Both statements are false

62 What will be the control objective for the risk given below?

Risk: Sales are recorded in the incorrect customer account.

- A Money received is recorded and banked
- B Fulfil all orders correctly
- C Credit notes are only raised for valid reasons
- D Invoices are recorded correctly in receivables

63 What will be the control objective for the risk given below?

Risk: Payment is stolen

- A Money received is recorded and banked
- B Fulfil all orders correctly
- C Credit notes are only raised for valid reasons
- D Invoices are recorded correctly in receivables

MULTIPLE-CHOICE QUESTIONS : SECTION 1

64 Which of the following may be an appropriate control to mitigate the risk of a sales order being forgotten?

- A Carry out credit checks for all customers
- B All orders are confirmed in writing
- C Arithmetic check on invoices
- D All credit notes are authorised

65 Which of the following may be an appropriate control to mitigate the risk of incorrect goods dispatched to the customer?

- A Goods dispatch notes prepared from order form
- B Credit limits applied and adhered to
- C Credit notes matched to original invoice
- D Open order file, which is regularly checked

66 Which of the following would be an appropriate test for the following control on sales?

Control: New orders only accepted if customer credit limit not breached.

- A Observe whether it is possible to over-ride credit limits
- B Review a sample of credit notes and ensure appropriate authorisation is in place
- C Using CAATs, test invoices for missing numbers
- D Review outstanding order list for old, uncleared items and obtain explanation

67 Which of the following would be an appropriate test for the following control on sales?

Control: Segregation of duties between receiving, recording and banking cash.

- A Observe whether it is possible to over-ride credit limits
- B Observe the procedures for receiving, recording and banking cash
- C For a sample of invoices review the numbering to ensure sequential
- D Review outstanding order list for old, uncleared items and obtain explanation

68 Are the following statements true or false?

1 Risks are things that could go wrong.
2 Control objectives are procedures put in place by an organisation to manage their risks.
3 A key risk in the purchasing cycle is the unauthorised procurement of goods or services.

- A 1 and 2 are true and 3 is false
- B 1 and 3 are true and 2 is false
- C 2 and 3 are true and 1 is false
- D All 3 are true

FAU: FOUNDATIONS IN AUDIT

69 Which of the following situations could lead to an invoice being paid twice?

1 Invoice is recorded in the payables ledger, not marked as 'posted' and put back into the 'to be processed' pile.

2 Payment of an invoice is not recorded as such in the payables ledger before the next round of payments is made.

3 Invoice is marked as paid immediately and a cheque is raised to clear the debt.

A 1 and 2

B 2 and 3

C 1 and 3

D All 3

70 Which of the following controls would help prevent or identify an invoice paid twice?

1 Supplier statement reconciliation.

2 Director's review of electronic bank transfer report.

3 Matching Goods Received Notes to invoices.

4 All outstanding orders kept on file for chasing.

A 1 and 2 only

B 1, 2 and 4 only

C 1, 2 and 3 only

D 1 and 3 only

71 What will be the control procedures for the risk given below?

Risk: Most advantageous terms from suppliers not obtained.

A Central ordering department set-up to take advantage of bulk discounts

B Goods arrival area kept secure

C Managers authorisation required before orders placed

D Purchase invoice matched to the goods received note

72 What will be the control procedure for the risk given below?

Risk: Fake supplier entered onto payables ledger.

A Central ordering department set-up to take advantage of bulk discounts

B Authorisation required for new suppliers

C Managers authorisation required before orders placed

D Goods arrival area kept secure

73 Which of the following would be an appropriate test for the following control on purchases?

Control: Supplier statements reconciled monthly.

A   For a sample of invoices, check they are matched to appropriate GRN

B   Check a selection of orders to ensure managers authorisation has been obtained

C   For the top 10 suppliers, obtain supplier statement reconciliations, ensure evidence of review, re-perform and follow up discrepancies

D   Obtain list of new suppliers added to payables ledger and check appropriate authorisation in place

74 Which of the following would be an appropriate test for the following control on purchases?

Control: Authorisation required for new suppliers.

A   For a sample of invoices, check they are matched to appropriate GRN

B   Check a selection of orders to ensure managers authorisation has been obtained

C   For the top 10 suppliers, obtain supplier statement reconciliations, ensure evidence of review, re-perform follow up discrepancies

D   Obtain list of new suppliers added to payables ledger and check appropriate authorisation in place

75 Are the following statements true or false?

1   Payroll systems include the maintenance of employee records.

2   Payment of wages and salaries is a key component of a payroll system.

A   1 is true and 2 is false

B   2 is true and 1 is false

C   Both statements are true

D   Both statements are false

76 Which of the following are risks which might occur in a payroll system?

1   Employee paid too much.

2   Employee paid too little.

3   Directors think they deserve a pay rise.

4   Tax liability paid late.

A   1, 2 and 3

B   1, 2 and 4

C   2, 3 and 4

D   1, 2, 3 and 4

77 Which of these controls can minimise the risk of cash wages being stolen?

- A Employee counts wages, and signs for them
- B Only actual employee can receive and sign for wages
- C Uncollected wages kept in safe until collection
- D All of the above

78 Which of the tests listed would be appropriate for the following control?

Control: Payment instructions are authorised by 2 members of the senior management team.

- A For a sample of payment instructions made, check that all have been authorised by 2 members of the senior management team
- B Check that amount paid agrees with timesheet
- C For a sample of pay amendments, ensure supporting documentation is available
- D Check that reconciliations have been performed for each month of the period under review

79 Which of the following are components of internal controls in accordance with ISA 315 (Revised) *Identifying and assessing the risks of material misstatement through understanding the entity and its environment*?

1. Control environment
2. Monitoring of controls
3. Information system
4. Control activities

- A 1, 2, and 3 only
- B 1, 2, and 4 only
- C 2, 3, and 4 only
- D 1, 2, 3, and 4

80 Which of the following cannot be considered a limitation of internal controls?

- A There are always chances of human errors
- B Management can collude to commit fraud
- C Controls are only for routine transactions
- D Effective controls increase the chances of fraud detection

81 Once the deficiencies have been identified in controls, what is the next course of action for the auditors?

- A Begin substantive testing immediately
- B Report deficiencies to the management in the form of a management letter
- C Re-design the controls for the management
- D Mention the control deficiencies in the audit report

MULTIPLE-CHOICE QUESTIONS : SECTION 1

82 Which of the following statements regarding the use of analytical procedures is incorrect?

- A It is carried out at planning stage to identify risks, decide nature, timing and extent of procedures
- B It is carried out during detailed testing to test financial statement assertions
- C It is carried out at review stage to see if audit objectives have been achieved
- D It is carried out once the audit report has been issued to confirm the validity of the audit opinion

83 The PRIMARY purpose of an auditor evaluating and testing the internal controls of a limited company is to enable the auditor to advise management of the deficiencies in the internal controls.

Is this statement true or false?

- A True.
- B False.

AUDIT EVIDENCE (INCLUDING COMPUTER-BASED SYSTEMS) AND SAMPLING

84 Which of the following financial statements assertions is NOT suitable for testing when the auditor wants to determine if a trade receivable balance should be in the financial statements at all?

- A Occurrence
- B Existence
- C Rights and obligation
- D Accuracy, valuation and allocation

85 Which of the following assertions will the auditors test if they want to see if there are any further liabilities that need to be included in the financial statements?

- A Completeness
- B Existence
- C Classification
- D Accuracy, valuation and allocation

86 Which of the following would be the most appropriate test for testing the existence of a non-current asset?

- A Inspect evidence of ownership
- B Inspect date on the invoice
- C Look for payment made to supplier
- D Physical verification of the asset

87 Which of the following is not an appropriate procedure when testing controls over payroll?

- A Carry out third party confirmation
- B Inspect authorised pay rates
- C Verify employees are genuine through contracts of employment.
- D Check tax and other deductions

88 Which of the following is the least reliable source of evidence for an auditor?

- A Recalculation of the depreciation charge by the auditor
- B Bank confirmation letter
- C Written representation letter
- D Re-performance of the bank reconciliation

89 When can 'a confirmation letter' not be used as evidence?

- A Circularisation of receivables
- B Confirmation of bank balances
- C Confirmation from legal advisers of actual or contingent liabilities arising from legal proceedings
- D Confirmation of inventory held at a client

90 Which of the following statements regarding the reliability of evidence are false?

1. Oral evidence is better than written.
2. Original documents are better than photocopies.
3. Internally generated evidence is better than independent external evidence.

- A 1 and 2 are false
- B 2 and 3 are false
- C 1 and 3 are false
- D All 3 statements are false

91 Which of the following statements is incorrect regarding sampling?

- A 100% testing may be appropriate in certain circumstances – particularly where there is a small population of high-value items.
- B There is no requirement to use sampling specified in any International Standards on Auditing ISAs).
- C At least 50% of each account balance has to be tested while selecting a sample.
- D Sampling involves the application of audit procedures to less than 100% of items within a class of transactions or account balance such that all sampling units have a chance of selection.

92 Which method of sampling is being described in the statement below?

'There is a constant interval between items selected (with a random start)'

- A Random sampling
- B Stratified sampling
- C Systematic sampling
- D Block sampling

93 Which of the following should give an auditor the STRONGEST assurance as to the truth and fairness of the receivables balance?

- A Carrying out positive circularisation of receivables balances in respect of year-end balances.
- B Carrying out negative circularisation of receivables balances in respect of year-end balances.
- C Confirming receivables balances by agreeing to sales invoices, authorised delivery notes and valid orders.
- D Confirming receivables balances by verifying subsequent payments after the year-end.

94 The auditor of Berry Co, a manufacturing company, has noted an increase in total sales value but a decrease in the company's gross profit percentage for 20X5 as compared to the previous year.

Which of the following is consistent with, and adequately explaining, the decrease?

1. Sales volumes have decreased as compared to 20X4.
2. During 20X5, due to a scarcity of supply the company had to pay higher prices when purchasing components.
3. During 20X5, a major component supplier withdrew early settlement discounts previously granted.

- A 1 only
- B 1 and 2
- C 2 only
- D 3 only

95 An auditor's responsibility extends to both evaluating the overall presentation of the financial statements and evaluating the reasonableness of accounting estimates made by management. Is this statement true or false?

- A True
- B False

96 Which of the following statements are true with regards to receivables' circularisation?

1 A positive confirmation would state the balance owed by the receivables and would ask them to confirm it.

2 A negative confirmation is one where the customer is asked to respond only if they disagree with the stated balance.

3 A non-reply in case of a negative confirmation can be misinterpreted to conclude that the receivable agrees with the balance whereas in reality, the receivable may simply not have received the letter or replied at all.

A Only 1 is true

B 1 and 2 are true

C 2 and 3 are true

D All three are true

97 Which of the following is not true regarding testing assertions on inventories?

A Completeness can be tested through an inventory count

B Valuation can be tested through an obsolescence review

C Existence can be tested through NRV tests

D Rights and obligation can be tested through a cut-off test

98 Which of the following are accounting estimates?

1 Inventory provisions

2 Depreciation rates

3 Accrued revenue

4 Profits/ losses on long term contract work

A 1 and 2

B 2 only

C 1, 2 and 4

D 1, 2, 3 and 4

99 Which of the following analytical procedures cannot be used in the audit of purchases?

A Comparison of current to prior year

B Comparison to budget

C Comparison by major supply

D Calculation of receivable days

100 You are performing a review of Panacure Co's accounts.

Which of the following balances will require the greatest amount of evidence?

- A Payables as it is the largest figure on the statement of financial position
- B Provisions as it is an estimate
- C Cash as the company has an overdraft
- D Cannot say as it depends on materiality and risk

101 You are planning the audit of the inventory and work-in-progress section for Helis Co.

Which of the following cannot be a suitable source of evidence?

- A Test count details performed at stock take
- B Review of the timesheets of the warehouse staff
- C Confirmations of inventories held by third parties
- D Previous years working papers

102 Which of the following is true regarding sampling?

1. Audit testing must cover 100% of transactions.
2. Increased risk in an area will result in an increase in size of sample tested.

- A 1 only
- B 2 only
- C Both
- D Neither

103 Which (if any) of the following would be risk(s) of misstatement that an auditor should be aware of when auditing the intangible non-current assets balance?

1. Expenses being capitalised as non-current assets inappropriately.
2. Intangible assets being carried at the wrong cost or valuation due to inflating the cost or valuation.

- A 1 only
- B 2 only
- C Both
- D Neither

104 While at the inventory count, an auditor should carry out 2 way testing.

Which of the following statements are true regarding 2 way testing?

1 Test is performed in 2 directions to test for valuation.

2 It involves selecting a sample from the inventory records and checking to the physical inventory.

3 It also involves selecting a sample from the physical inventory and checking it to the inventory records.

A 1 and 2

B 1 and 3

C 2 and 3

D 1, 2 and 3

105 Inventories are normally a high risk element in an audit and the auditor is particularly concerned with the valuation of closing inventories.

Which of the following statements are true regarding closing inventories?

1 Inventory is included in the financial statements at the higher of cost and NRV.

2 If obsolete inventory continues to be included in the inventory valuation at cost, when the NRV is actually much lower, stock is overvalued.

A 1 only

B 2 only

C 1 and 2

D Neither statement is true

106 Whilst carrying out test counts at a toy manufacturing company, early January, Alan notices a large number of boxes on a high shelf, covered with a thick layer of dust. Review of the inventory listing showed these goods were valued at full cost.

What risk would you identify in this scenario?

A Inventory is undervalued

B Inventory is overvalued

C The quantity of inventory is incorrect

D Inventory has been included at lower of cost and net realisable value

107 Whilst attending an inventory count at a car parts manufacturer, Isabella noticed that the count sheets supplied to counters had the expected values already marked on them.

What is the risk in this situation?

A Inventory is valued at lower of cost and net realisable value

B Two-way testing has not been carried out by the auditor

C Counters make assumptions of how many items there are, rather than actually counting

D There is no risk in this situation

108 Which of the following statements are false with regards to inventory count?

　　A　Attendance at inventory counts can bring to light obsolescence issues

　　B　Where client has counted inventory, auditor can assume values are correct

　　C　Auditors should always query things that look unusual even if they are the not the focus of a test count

　　D　The auditor should ensure that the person in charge of routine inventory control is not the one carrying out the inventory count

109 Which of the following is least likely to be the reason why a returned customer receivables confirmation may show a different amount to the one in the receivables ledger?

　　A　Timing differences – cash/invoices in transit

　　B　Cut-off issues

　　C　Teeming and lading or other theft/fraud

　　D　Incorrect aging of that trade receivables

110 Which of the following is least likely to be the main information source for testing cash and bank balances?

　　A　Cash book

　　B　Bank statements

　　C　Sales and purchase day book

　　D　Bank letters

111 Which of the following statements is true regarding the audit of cash and bank balances?

　　A　Raising cheques pre-year end has the effect of improving the current ratio

　　B　Bank confirmation letters are a weak source of audit evidence

　　C　Petty cash should always be counted

　　D　Petty cash is normally the most risky area in an audit

112 Which of the following is true regarding the audit of liabilities?

　　A　Greatest risk with liabilities is overstatement

　　B　Supplier statements are a good source of audit evidence

　　C　All suppliers send statements on a regular basis

　　D　The supplier statements are the only source of evidence required to carry out supplier statement reconciliations

113 Which of the following financial statement assertions may not be appropriate for a statement of comprehensive income (profit and loss) balance?

- A Completeness
- B Occurrence
- C Rights and obligation
- D Cut-off

114 Which of the following circumstances would require comparatively lesser evidence if considered in terms of sufficiency of evidence?

- A If evidence available is highly reliable
- B If the client is a new business and first year's financial statements are being audited
- C If the internal controls are weak
- D If it is a complex balance for example work in process

115 Which of the following are audit procedures in accordance with ISA 500?

1 Confirmation
2 Re-performance/recalculation
3 Inspection

- A 1 and 2
- B 1 and 3
- C 2 and 3
- D 1, 2 and 3

116 Which of the following functions are least likely to be performed by audit software?

- A Highlight trends
- B Sequence checks
- C Review of staff competence
- D Highlighting by exception

117 Which of the following is incorrect regarding application controls?

- A Application controls are controls on transactions and data
- B Application controls ensure that data is valid, accurate and complete
- C Example of application controls include administration and structure of the information system
- D Examples of application controls are batch controls, encryption, data input controls etc.

118 Test data is a computer assisted audit technique (CAAT) where the auditor generates data and processes it using the client's computer system.

Which of the following statements is incorrect regarding test data?

A Test data ensures that programmed controls work effectively.

B Test data should contain data of both valid and invalid nature.

C The auditor can use 'live' test data or 'dead' test data.

D Discrepancies between predicted and actual results must only be documented and resolved if the financial amounts involved are material.

119 When determining the sample size, auditors should consider various factors.

Which of the following relationships between the sample size and these factors is incorrect?

A For a high risk area, the sample size will be large

B For a low risk area, the sample size will be small

C For a small tolerable misstatement, the sample size will be large

D For a large tolerable misstatement, the sample size will be large

120 Which of the following statements is true for the following scenario?

Tolerable misstatement:	$75
Population monetary value:	$10,000
Sample selected from the population:	$2,500
Error found in the sample:	$42

A It can be concluded that the population is fairly stated

B Total misstatement in the population are less than the tolerable misstatement

C Total errors in the population are more than the tolerable misstatement

D No further audit work is required for this population

121 Which of the following is a situation where the net realisable value may be less than cost?

A Selling at a profit

B Less costs of manufacture

C Reduced selling price of products

D No buying and production errors

122 The auditors have circularised Robin and Co's receivables balances and have received a reply that indicates that the customer disagrees with the balance circularised. The auditor is attempting to reconcile the balance.

Which of the following can be possible reconciling items?

1   Cash in transit.

2   Credit notes not yet recorded.

3   Goods in transit.

A   1 and 2

B   1 and 3

C   2 and 3

D   1, 2 and 3

123 **Which of the following CANNOT lead to the receivables balance being overstated?**

A   Sales invoices posted twice

B   Sales invoice omitted

C   Cash received not recorded

D   Credit note omitted

AUDIT COMPLETION

124 **Which of the following statements are incorrect regarding audit review procedures?**

1   In a cold review, the working papers produced by the audit staff are checked by a more experienced member of the audit team.

2   In a hot review, the audit file and final accounts are reviewed by a manager or partner before the audit report is signed.

3   A peer review is one in which one firm of auditors reviews the working papers of another firm.

A   1 and 2

B   1 and 3

C   2 and 3

D   1, 2 and 3

125 Subsequent events are events occurring and facts discovered between the period end and the date the financial statements are authorised for issue.

Which of the following applies to the statements given below?

1 A disclosure may need to be made for non-adjusting events.

2 A fire in a warehouse in the week immediately after the reporting date destroyed all the company's inventory. This is a non-adjusting event.

3 The company has a factory in an overseas country where a coup d'état takes place early in the new financial period and all the company's assets are nationalised. This is an adjusting event.

A 1 and 2 are true

B 2 and 3 are true

C 1 and 3 are true

D All 3 are true

126 Which stages of the audit can analytical procedures be used in?

1 Planning

2 Detailed testing

3 Review

A 1 and 2 only

B 1 and 3 only

C 2 and 3 only

D 1, 2 and 3

127 What are the two types of internal review which a firm may undertake as part of their monitoring of quality control procedures?

A Hot review and cold review

B Going concern review and subsequent events review

C Going concern review and audit file review

D None of the above

128 Which of the following is least likely to be considered an indication of going concern problem if taken into account in isolation?

A Default on loan agreements

B Unplanned sales of a large number of non-current assets

C Major technological change in the industry

D A two percent decrease in the gross profit margin as compared to last year

129 You are responsible for the audit of Mowbray Computers Co.

The company assembles microcomputers from components purchased from the Far East and sells them to major retailers and to individuals and businesses.

In the current year, there has been a recession and strong competition which has resulted in a fall in sales and gross profit margin. This has led to a trading loss and the company experiencing cash flow problems.

Which of the following can be considered as an indication that Mowbray is facing going concern problems?

1   Fall in sales due to recession and stiff competition.

2   Fall in GP margin and trading loss.

3   Certain microcomputers may be obsolete.

A   1 and 2

B   1 and 2

C   2 and 3

D   1, 2 and 3

130 **Which of the following statements is incorrect regarding going concern review?**

A   Auditors assess the company's ability to continue as going concern and directors satisfy themselves that the use of the going concern basis of accounting is reasonable and disclosures made adequate

B   There are no disclosure implications if the company is a going concern

C   If there are going concern problems, the doubts and their effect have to be disclosed

D   If there are going concern problems, the basis on which the financial statements have been prepared have to be disclosed

131 **Which of the following are typical matters for which auditors normally get written representations?**

1   Confirmation that the directors believe the company to be a going concern for the foreseeable future.

2   Confirmation that all books, records, information and explanations have been supplied to the auditors.

3   Confirmation that there are no contingent liabilities other than those disclosed to the auditors.

4   Explanation of reasons why errors passed on by the auditors have not been adjusted.

A   1, 2 and 3 only

B   1, 2 and 4 only

C   2, 3 and 4 only

D   1, 2, 3 and 4

132 The financial statements for the year ended 31 December 20X5 are being audited.

Which of the following would be a non-adjusting event?

- A Trade receivables may 'go bad', resulting in additional provisions or write-offs
- B Final dividend is declared
- C Inventory may be sold at less than cost
- D Sales revenue returns may indicate problems with year-end inventory holdings

133 You are about to undertake the audit of Rushley Co. This is the first year of trading for the company. The owner of Rushley has mentioned during your recent meeting that he will be 'leaving it to the auditors to sort out' whether he has been calculating PAYE/NI properly as he doesn't really have much experience in this area. He has kept 'rough workings' as to how he arrived at his figures, but nothing more.

Which of the following could be a possible implication of this for your audit report?

- A As directors are not responsible for keeping proper accounting records, this will not have any impact on the audit report
- B This is a common occurrence for audits and does not limit our scope
- C If the director is unable to provide evidence to support the PAYE/NI calculations, then the auditor will be required to produce a qualified opinion
- D This is immaterial and so it will not affect the audit report

134 The auditor needs to carry out a going concern review before the audit opinion is issued.

Which of the following is least likely to be considered a going concern review procedure?

- A Review post year end management accounts to analyse trend in performance
- B Review post year-end events to determine whether they are adjusting or non-adjusting
- C Review cash flow forecasts for evidence of expected improvement or deterioration in the coming year
- D Consult management about future intentions and obtain written representations if required

135 For the situation given below, which audit opinion would be the most appropriate?

'No inventory count carried out at a branch. Inventory is both material and pervasive to the accounts.'

- A Qualified opinion
- B Disclaimer of opinion
- C Adverse opinion
- D Unmodified opinion.

136 For the situation given below, which audit opinion would be the most appropriate?

'Destruction of accounting records relating to an area pervasive to the accounts.'

A Unmodified opinion

B Adverse opinion

C Disclaimer of opinion

D Qualified opinion

137 For the situation given below, which audit opinion would be the most appropriate?

'Difference of opinion between directors and auditor as to whether to provide for a material doubtful debt.'

A Qualified opinion

B Adverse opinion

C Unmodified opinion

D Disclaimer of opinion

138 For the situation given below, which audit opinion would be the most appropriate?

Inappropriate basis of preparation used for example if the going concern basis has been used when the break up basis should have been used.

A Unmodified opinion

B Adverse opinion

C Disclaimer of opinion

D Qualified opinion

139 Which of the following statements is TRUE with regard to an emphasis of matter paragraph included in a modified auditor's report?

1 The paragraph may refer to a matter other than those presented or disclosed in the financial statements that, in the auditor's opinion are relevant to users' understanding of the audit.

2 The paragraph should ordinarily refer to the fact that the auditor's opinion is modified in respect of the subject matter.

3 The inclusion of the paragraph should not affect the auditor's opinion on the financial statements.

A 1 only

B 2 only

C 3 only

D 1, 2 and 3

Section 2

PRACTICE QUESTIONS

THE BUSINESS ENVIRONMENT

1 ADVANTAGES OF AUDIT

(a) Only certain types of entities are legally required to have an audit; others may choose to do so.

You are required to discuss the advantages of an audit for different types of entity.
(10 marks)

(b) **Describe the limitations of the external audit in relation to the detection and reporting of fraud.** **(5 marks)**

(Total: 15 marks)

2 X CO

You are the manager of the audit team which has recently completed the audit of X Co, a shoe manufacturing and importing limited liability company, which has one central factory and warehouse and 32 retail branches spread throughout the country and which only receive inventory from the central warehouse. All accounting records are maintained at the head office which is on the same site as the factory and warehouse. Control of the branches is achieved by recording all inventory movements and sales at selling price.

An example of a week's transactions would be as follows:

	All at selling price $
Opening inventory at branch	25,000
Transfers to branch from warehouse	14,500
Sales for week (cash banked)	(15,000)
Closing inventory counted by branch staff or external counters	24,500

Since opening inventory, transfers from warehouse and revenue (cash banked) are all known, the theoretical closing inventory can easily be calculated and compared with that actually counted to establish gains or losses. X Co uses an external company specialising in inventory management and part of their work is to observe inventory counts at branches on a rotational basis. You have reviewed the work of the external counters and have satisfied yourself that it is an effective tool of management and that it forms a reliable part of the whole system of internal control.

KAPLAN PUBLISHING

The company's total year-end inventory in the central warehouse and branches is valued at $2.6 million and each branch holds between $20,000 and $30,000 of inventory. The audit team has tested the existence and satisfactory operation of internal controls by visiting 10 branches. The audit team attended the factory/warehouse inventory count and the inventory count at a further 10 branches (the 10 being chosen out of the 32 on a rotational basis). You had concluded that the inventory counting was carried out satisfactorily and you were of the opinion (at the close of the audit field work) that the company's inventory was fairly valued. Prior to the partner in charge of the audit signing the audit opinion, the Finance Director of the company telephoned to say that the external counters had found that the physical inventory at one branch was less than the book quantities and the manager had admitted misappropriating company footwear and falsifying the inventory records.

You had carried out tests on the internal controls at the branch which was subject to audit during the year. The Finance Director is of the opinion that, while the theft is not material in the context of this year's financial statements, your firm has been negligent in its audit approach.

Required:

The Finance Director wishes to meet with you to discuss the issues; he has also asked you to prepare an executive summary, rather than a full report outlining the auditor's duty to detect fraud, and relate your report to the situation that has occurred within X Co.

Note: this question is longer and more detailed than you are likely to experience in the exam, but is a good question to aid revision. **(10 marks)**

3 LIMITATION OF LIABILITY OF AUDITORS

It has been suggested that the liability of auditors should be limited due to two factors:

(1) the increasing number and size of damages claims being brought against auditors;

(2) the difficulty in obtaining adequate professional indemnity insurance cover, and its cost.

Required:

(a) Briefly describe the ways the liability of auditors could be limited, and consider the practicality of these methods of limiting an auditor's liability. **(4 marks)**

(b) Consider what the effect of limiting an auditor's liability is likely to have on:

　(i) the investor's view of the reliability of the audit opinion; and

　(ii) the amount of work an auditor will perform (compared with the work he would perform if his liability were unlimited), and the effect this will have on the reliability of the audit opinion. **(2 marks)**

(c) Briefly come to a conclusion on:

　(i) whether you consider it is practicable for an auditor's liability to be limited

　(ii) whether limiting an auditor's liability will affect the reliability of the audit opinion; and

　(iii) whether you would agree with the proposal that an auditor's liability should be limited. **(4 marks)**

(Total: 10 marks)

4 EXTERNAL AUDITORS

The responsibilities of external auditors are not always well understood, especially with regard to the detection and reporting of fraud. When external auditors provide non-audit services to their audit clients, it is essential that the auditors make a clear distinction between their audit and non-audit responsibilities.

Required:

(a) Explain why it is essential for external auditors to be independent of their clients.

(5 marks)

(b) Explain the advantages and disadvantages of external auditors providing consulting services to their audit clients. (5 marks)

(Total: 10 marks)

5 EXTERNAL AUDITOR RESPONSIBILITIES

The responsibilities of external auditors are not always well understood, especially with regard to directors and shareholders.

Required:

Explain the responsibilities of external auditors to directors and shareholders.

(Total: 6 marks)

THE AUDIT FRAMEWORK

6 EAGLE CO

When carrying out audit sampling auditors need to consider whether to use statistical sampling.

Required:

(i) Define the term 'audit sampling'. (2 marks)

(ii) State FOUR advantages of using statistical sampling rather than non-statistical sampling (judgemental sampling). (4 marks)

(Total: 6 marks)

7 SPARROW CO

For recurring audits it is advisable to split working papers between permanent and current audit files, and in many firms working papers on the current audit file are automated.

Required:

List SIX examples of the working papers ordinarily contained in a current audit file.

(Total: 6 marks)

8 ETHICS

(a) Respecting the confidentiality of clients' business and financial affairs is of fundamental importance to the auditor. However, there may be occasions when it is necessary to override this principle and make disclose of matters that would normally be regarded as confidential.

Required:

State the exceptions to the general principle that confidentially should be maintained of clients' business and financial affairs. (5 marks)

(b) It is important for firms of auditors to maintain good ethical practices.

Required:

Explain the mechanisms that a firm of professional accountants may put in place to ensure that they uphold good ethical practices. (5 marks)

(c) In relation to professional ethics, the 'advocacy threat' is regarded as a threat to the objectivity and independence that auditors should safeguard against when agreeing to perform work and services on behalf of clients.

Required:

Explain the nature of the advocacy threat in relation to independence and objectivity of auditors. (5 marks)

(Total: 15 marks)

9 FASTBIKES

You are the audit partner responsible for the audit of the accounts of Fastbikes, a limited liability company, manufacturing bicycles for the home and overseas markets.

As part of the audit planning process, you have been asked by the audit appointment partner to prepare briefing notes so that less experienced members of the audit team understand some of the relevant issues regarding auditor appointment etc.

Required:

Prepare briefing notes relating to the position of the external auditor which deal with the following issues:

(i) eligibility to act

(ii) security of tenure

(iii) primary objective and the limitations on the scope of the auditor's work in order to achieve this objective.

(Total: 10 marks)

PRACTICE QUESTIONS : SECTION 2

10 SUJON

Following your firm's audit of the financial statements of Sujon, a limited liability company, you have received a letter from the company's managing director. An extract from the letter reads as follows:

'It was pleasing to see that you consider that our company has a strong control environment. We wish to consider further your firm's view that the company could benefit from the introduction of an internal audit department. The scope of activities of such a department is wide and we understand that your firm may be able to use some of the department's work to reduce the level of your audit procedures. Similarly we understand that your firm may be able to advise us on recruitment for an internal audit department. We shall be obliged if the partner responsible for the audit of our company's financial statements will attend our next board meeting to advise on these points in more detail.'

Required:

(a) **Explain what is meant by the term 'strong control environment'.** (4 marks)

(b) **Briefly discuss whether a meeting with the directors as suggested would compromise your firm's audit independence.** (6 marks)

(Total: 10 marks)

11 RESPONSIBILITIES REGARDING FRAUD

Whilst there is a difference between the roles of internal auditors and external (registered) auditors, they often liaise on various matters and a Chartered Certified Accountant employed in either capacity has an obligation to adhere to the Fundamental Principles of the Code of ethics as set out in ACCA's Rules of Professional Conduct.

Required:

Discuss the extent to which external auditors should be expected to detect and report fraud.

(Total: 6 marks)

12 AUDIT PROGRAMMES

You are an audit partner for a firm of accountants and you have specific responsibility for quality control issues within the firm.

Required:

Prepare briefing notes that can be distributed to the partners in the firm which list the respective advantages and disadvantages of using standard audit programmes.

(Total: 6 marks)

13 INDEPENDENCE PROBLEMS

Provided an auditor possesses professional objectivity, he does not have to be *seen* to be independent.

Required:

Comment on the above statement ensuring that you include an explanation of the term 'professional objectivity' and include commentary on the validity of the statement.

(Total: 6 marks)

FAU: FOUNDATIONS IN AUDIT

14 VISWA

Viswa is a company that provides call centre services for a variety of organisations. It operates in a medium sized city in which yours is the largest audit firm. Viswa is owned and run by two entrepreneurs with experience in this sector and has been in existence for five years. It is expanding rapidly in terms of its client base, the number of staff it employs and its profits. It is now 15 June 20X4 and you have been approached to perform the audit for the year ending 30 June 20X4.

Required:

(a) Explain the respective duties of directors and of auditors should your firm accept appointment as auditor to Viswa. **(10 marks)**

Viswa is considering establishing an internal audit department next year. The finance director has asked whether the work performed by the internal audit department can be relied upon by your audit firm.

(b) Explain the factors that should be considered by an external auditor before reliance can be placed on the work performed by a company's internal audit department.

(5 marks)

(Total: 15 marks)

15 AUDIT WORKING PAPERS

You have been asked to make a presentation to colleagues in your firm on audit working papers.

Required:

In readiness for the presentation:

(i) Explain the difference between a permanent audit file and a current audit file.

(2 marks)

(ii) Give FOUR examples of matters that should be recorded in EACH file, with regard to the audit of the financial statements of a company. **(8 marks)**

(Total: 10 marks)

16 P AND PARTNERS

As a consultant on auditing issues you have been asked by P and Partners, a firm of Registered Auditors, to advise them on quality control procedures.

The firm is recently established and has offices at 1 High Street, Lowtown. It has three partners, three qualified staff, 16 unqualified audit staff and four secretarial staff. They rely heavily on information technology and use various auditing spreadsheets and word processing software packages in their day-to-day activities. The firm has numerous audit clients across a range of activities but specialises in the audit of accounts of companies trading as Travel Agents. Whilst most of the detailed audit work is carried out by unqualified staff, each audit assignment is controlled by a partner and supervised by a qualified member of the audit staff. The partners are particularly concerned that they may have poor procedures with regard to:

(i) ensuring that staff are competent to carry out their work efficiently

(ii) the preparation and review of audit working papers.

PRACTICE QUESTIONS : SECTION 2

Required:

(a) State briefly why it is important for an audit firm to have good quality control procedures across its range of activities. **(3 marks)**

(b) State why it is important that an audit firm should prepare audit working papers and comment on TWO reasons why these need to be complete and sufficiently detailed. **(3 marks)**

(Total: 6 marks)

AUDIT PLANNING AND RISK

17 FINCH CO

Finch Co operates eight hotels in various locations around the country. The following information relates to the company's operations during the year ended 30 November 20X7.

1 Following career moves by the ex-managing director and the ex-financial director, two replacement directors were appointed in February 2007. The new managing director has extensive experience of working in the hotel sector and adopts an aggressive management style whilst the new financial director is an unqualified accountant with only limited experience in the hotel sector.

2 The company's directors, central administration and accounts department are located at its head office premises and wages payments to all employees together with all company supplier payments are made from there. Accounts staff at each hotel deposit hotel takings into the company's bank account at their local branch of the bank.

3 The company's accounting system, which comprises fully integrated general, trade payables and trade receivables ledgers, relies on daily sales and accounting information being input into remote terminals at each hotel, for transfer to a secure central computer based in the head office accounts department. The new financial director has changed some of the general controls of the system including those relating to the use of the remote terminals.

4 The company operates a cash or bank card payment policy for non-corporate customers with credit terms being offered only to corporate customers.

5 The remuneration package of each of the company's directors provides for the payment of a bonus based on the profits of the company. Similarly, the remuneration package of each hotel general manager provides for a bonus based on the profits of their hotel.

6 Independent contractors were employed to construct a new hotel on land already owned by the company. Work commenced in January 20X7 and the new hotel began trading in November 20X7.

7 Each hotel offers restaurant, gym, conference and meeting facilities. The company owns all of the land and buildings. During the year, two of the hotels were extended substantially to create additional restaurant space, whilst a swimming pool was constructed at another.

8 In keeping with the company policy, all hotels are furnished and equipped similarly with ongoing repairs, maintenance and replacement programmes for furnishings and equipment.

9   In September 20X7, food poisoning at one of the company's largest hotels resulted in hospital admission for eight of the hotel's customers. The directors of Finch Co have received legal advice confirming that the company is likely to have to pay compensation to settle the legal claims that have been lodged against it in this regard.

Required:

(a) Explain the meaning of the term 'inherent risk'. (2 marks)

(b) State with reasons FIVE factors that would affect the initial assessment of the inherent risk associated with the audit of the financial statements of Finch Co for the year ended 30 November 20X7. (10 marks)

(c) Explain what is meant by the term 'general controls' as applied to a computer-based accounting system and state the objectives of such controls. (3 marks)

Note: this question is longer and more detailed than you are likely to experience in the exam, but is a good question to aid revision. (Total: 15 marks)

18   WILLIAMS

You are the manager responsible for the audit of Williams, a limited liability company, which manufactures magnetic media products.

You are planning the audit for the year ending 30 June 20X2. From your discussions with the finance director, you ascertain that during the year the company made a significant investment in equipment comprising a moulding machine and a conveyor system which have been included in the non-current asset register at $525,000.

The moulding machine is used to produce floppy disks and the conveyor system carries the disks from production to the packing department. The moulding machine was purchased on 1 March 20X2 from the manufacturer in Germany and the price was agreed in Euros, payable one half on 1 March 20X2 and the balance 60 days later.

The conveyor system was designed and constructed by the company's employees using components specifically bought in.

You also ascertain that the company's application for a government grant of $95,000 in respect of other non-current assets, acquired earlier in the year, has been submitted and approved. The expenditure relating to these non-current assets has already been verified as the company's grant application was reported on by your firm. However, the company had not received the grant at the time of your discussions with the finance director.

Required:

Prepare, for inclusion in an audit planning memorandum, a list of the potential risks of misstatement in respect of the above items and the steps that you would take to address them.

(Total: 15 marks)

23 MATERIALITY

You have been asked by the partner in charge of your firm to provide guidance to audit staff about materiality; he believes that if this guidance is provided to staff it will allow them to carry out audits more effectively.

Required:

(a) Define the term materiality (2 marks)

(b) Explain why it is important to auditors (4 marks)

(Total: 6 marks)

24 TIGHTROPE

You have recently completed the first audit of Tightrope, a limited liability company, and at the post audit meeting with the directors they express concern at the high level of audit fees. They ask you to review audit costs and explain to them how the costs might be reduced in future years. On reviewing the audit file you find that the following factors were influential on the cost of the audit:

(i) The company introduced a new category of non-current assets into its statement of financial position for the first time during the previous financial year.

(ii) The computerised accounting system had been upgraded during the year.

(iii) Several year-end suppliers' statements did not agree with the payables ledger balances, and an extensive payables circularisation was undertaken.

(iv) Prior to your appointment as auditor, the wages clerk had stolen company funds by falsifying the wages payroll.

Required:

(a) Explain to the directors why the above factors would lead to an increase in time spent on audit work. (8 marks)

(b) Discuss the view that the constant pressure exerted on auditors to reduce audit fees will result in a reduction in the efficiency and effectiveness of the audit.

(2 marks)

(Total: 10 marks)

25 AUDIT RISK

One of the recent developments in auditing has been consideration of audit risk, which in turn has influenced the way audits are carried out and the balance of work between the different sections of an audit.

Required:

List and describe the factors you would consider in assessing the audit risk when you are planning the audit of the accounts of a manufacturing company, and the situations when you consider there will be a high level of audit risk. Your answer should consider the following items in the accounts:

(i) tangible non-current assets

(ii) inventory

(iii) trade receivables

(iv) trade payables

(v) contingencies.

(Total: 15 marks)

26 BRAHMS CO

You have been assigned to your firm's audit of the financial statements of Brahms Co for the year ending 31 December 20X5. At the planning meeting, attended by all members of the audit team, the audit manager confirmed that the firm would adopt a risk-based approach to the audit.

Required:

Explain what is meant by the term 'a risk-based approach' to an audit. Your answer should also explain the audit risk model.

(Total: 6 marks)

27 MOZART CO

You have been assigned to your firm's audit of the financial statements of Mozart Co for the year ending 31 December 20X5.

At the planning meeting, attended by all members of the audit team, the audit manager confirmed that the firm would adopt a risk-based approach to the audit. The manager also explained the importance of preparing good audit working papers and confirmed that he expected every working paper to be properly completed.

Required:

Briefly explain the purpose of audit working papers and comment on the matters to be considered generally, in assessing the extent of working papers to be prepared.

(Total: 6 marks)

28 TULIP CO

Required:

(a) Identify and explain FOUR matters that an auditor should consider when evaluating the control environment of an entity. **(6 marks)**

(b) Your firm is about to tender for the appointment as auditors to Tulip Co, a company which provides adventure holidays for groups of school children.

Having had an initial meeting with the director of the company, John White, your firm's audit engagement partner, has established that the company has a good control environment.

Your firm has no previous experience of auditing a company engaged in the adventure holiday sector. However, John is confident that, by ensuring good audit planning, a thorough understanding of the business and properly directed substantive procedures, the firm will be able to carry out an efficient and effective audit of the financial statements of Tulip Co.

John has had discussions with the audit manager who would be assigned to the Tulip Co audit, and together they have decided that, if the tender is successful, the firm will use document flowcharts to record the company's accounting and internal control systems.

Required:

(i) Identify SIX areas of the business operations of Tulip Co on which your firm should obtain detailed knowledge, in order to obtain an understanding of the business, if it wins the tender for the audit of the company. **(6 marks)**

(iii) Identify THREE benefits of using document flowcharts to record a company's accounting and internal control systems. **(3 marks)**

(Total: 15 marks)

29 PARKER

You are the audit manager for Parker, a limited liability company which sells books, CDs, DVDs and similar items via two divisions: mail order and on-line ordering on the Internet.

Parker is a new audit client. You are commencing the planning of the audit for the year-ended 31 May 20X5. An initial meeting with the directors has provided the information below.

The company's sales revenue is in excess of $85 million with net profits of $4 million. All profits are currently earned in the mail order division, although the Internet division is expected to return a small net profit next year. Sales revenue is growing at the rate of 20% per annum and net profit has remained almost the same for the last four years. In the next year, the directors plan to expand the range of goods sold through the Internet division to include toys, garden furniture and fashion clothes. The directors believe that when one product has been sold on the Internet, then any other product can be as well.

The accounting system to record sales by the mail order division is relatively old. It relies on extensive manual input to transfer orders received in the post onto Parker's computer systems. Recently errors have been known to occur, in the input of orders, and in the invoicing of goods following despatch. The directors maintain that the accounting system produces materially correct figures and they cannot waste time in identifying relatively minor errors. The company accountant, who is not qualified and was appointed because he is a personal friend of the directors, agrees with this view.

The directors estimate that their expansion plans will require a bank loan of approximately $30 million, partly to finance the enhanced web site but also to provide working capital to increase inventory levels. A meeting with the bank has been scheduled for three months after the year end. The directors expect an unmodified auditor's report to be signed prior to this time.

Required:

Identify and describe the matters that give rise to audit risks associated with Parker.

(Total: 15 marks)

ACCOUNTING SYSTEMS AND CONTROLS (INCLUDING COMPUTER-BASED SYSTEMS)

GENERAL PRINCIPLES

30   DS

As the auditor in charge of the audit of the accounts of DS, a limited liability company, you are about to review the internal control systems of the company.

The company is long-established and operates three department stores. Each store has its own warehouse but the administration, buying and accounting operations are centrally located in the largest store. Your review will include a detailed examination of the control environment and of the control procedures employed by the company.

Required:

(a)   Explain in your own words the meaning of the term 'internal control system'.

(3 marks)

(b)   Identify THREE different categories of control procedures

and

for each category identified give ONE example of a specific procedure you would expect to find in the daily activities of DS. (12 marks)

(Total: 15 marks)

31 WOODS

Joy Lee is an inexperienced member of your audit team currently involved in the audit of the accounts of Woods, a limited liability company, for the year ended 31 May 20X8. The company is engaged in the manufacture and distribution of garden furniture. Joy is assisting in the audit of the non-current assets; however, given her limited experience, she is puzzled by some areas of the audit programme.

As you are the auditor in charge of the audit she has approached you for guidance on internal control objectives.

Required:

Prepare guidance notes, in any format, which give three internal control objectives of a non-current assets accounting system. For each objective give an example of a control that would help to achieve the objective.

(Total: 6 marks)

32 FOREST

Roy Race is an inexperienced member of your audit team currently involved in the audit of the accounts of Forest, a limited liability company, for the year ended 31 May 20X8. The company is engaged in the manufacture and distribution of garden furniture. Roy is assisting in the audit of sales and receivables of the company; however, given his limited experience, he is puzzled by some areas of the audit programme.

As you are the auditor in charge of the audit Roy has approached you for guidance on internal control objectives.

Required:

Prepare guidance notes, in any format, which give three internal control objectives of a sales and receivables accounting system. For each objective give an example of a control that would help to achieve the objective.

(Total: 6 marks)

33 SHOW

In May 20X3 three senior managers of Show, a limited liability company, were dismissed, following the discovery that, since November 20X2, they had colluded in diverting company funds to make relatively small fraudulent payments to one of the company's suppliers. The discovery was made during an annual review and detailed testing of accounting control procedures by the company's internal audit department.

The following extracts are taken from the internal audit department's report to the directors of the company in connection with this matter:

- 'The company's external auditors did not detect the fraud in their audit of the company's financial statements for the year ended 31 March 20X3 – this is perhaps understandable.'
- 'There are inherent limitations with any internal control system. These can be broadly categorised under five different headings.'

- 'We can carry out regular reviews and testing of the company's accounting control procedures. However, the extent to which the external auditors may depend upon the work of our department will depend on their evaluation of our work. This will involve the consideration of various factors.'
- 'We have ensured that there are now adequate internal check procedures throughout all areas of the company's accounting systems.'

Required:

(a) **Comment on the external auditors' responsibility with regard to the detection of fraud and from the information provided, explain why it was 'perhaps understandable' that they did not detect the fraud which was perpetrated against Show.** (6 marks)

(b) **State FOUR inherent limitations of any internal control system.** (4 marks)

(Total: 10 marks)

34 DOORS

Doors is a limited liability manufacturing company. The directors are aware of the need to maintain internal control systems in the company but are also aware of the inherent limitations of such systems.

To enhance the control environment of the company, an internal audit department has been established and its first task is to conduct a review of the internal controls relating to the accounting systems of the company.

As part of the review process the company accountant has been asked to complete an internal control questionnaire (ICQ).

Required:

(a) **Identify TWO objectives that internal controls relating to an accounting system should achieve.** (2 marks)

(b) **Discuss the significance of each of the following questions included in the ICQ to be completed by the company accountant of Doors.**

  (i) Are sales ledger balances periodically reviewed and subjected to appropriate action by credit control staff? (5 marks)

  (ii) Is plant and equipment owned by the company regularly inspected by independent company employees? (5 marks)

  (iii) Is the work of absent employees carried out in their absence by other employees? (3 marks)

(Total: 15 marks)

35 ROSE CO

Rose Co, a haulage contractor company with sales of $7 million and profits of $1 million for the financial year ended 31 January 20X6, recently dismissed its financial director for misappropriating company funds. Following his dismissal, the remaining directors of Rose Co asked your firm to carry out a full review of the company's internal control system with a view to recommending improvements as appropriate to guarantee the effectiveness of the controls.

An audit partner at your firm has written to the directors of Rose Co confirming that the firm will review the various components of the company's internal controls, including control activities employed. He has explained, however, that any system of internal control can only provide reasonable assurance that the company's financial reporting objectives will be achieved.

The company has over 1,500 customers to whom it sells on credit terms and it employs a manager and five clerks in its sales accounting function. The circumstances of the financial director's dismissal were that, in the six-month period up to 31 October 20X5, he colluded with another senior manager of the company, to misappropriate individual sums totalling $9,682 received from the company's customers. The directors discovered the fraud following a meeting between one of the customers and the managing director of Rose Co in April 20X6, and have subsequently asserted that the auditors of Rose Co were negligent in not having discovered the fraud whilst auditing the company's financial statements for the year ended 31 January 20X6. The auditors have stated that the directors are being unreasonable in making this assertion and are confident that an independent review of their audit working papers will confirm that they have not been negligent in their audit work.

Required:

(a) Explain why it is important that the directors of Rose Co should ensure that the company has an effective system of internal control. **(3 marks)**

(b) Explain why any system of internal control can provide an entity with only reasonable assurance that the entity's financial reporting objectives will be achieved. **(8 marks)**

(c) Briefly comment as to whether the directors of Rose Co would appear to be justified in asserting that the company's auditors were negligent in not detecting the fraud perpetrated by the company's financial director and another senior manager during the year ended 31 January 20X6. **(4 marks)**

(Total: 15 marks)

ASCERTAINING AND RECORDING THE SYSTEM

36 HOCATTA

You have been assigned to the interim audit of Hocatta, a limited liability company, a retailer of motorcycles and a longstanding audit client. Operating from a large retail and office unit, the company sells both new and used motorcycles. The average inventory holding of motorcycles throughout the year is 600 units with a total cost of approximately $4 million.

During the current financial year the company has made major changes to its motorcycle purchase and inventory systems. One of your first tasks during the interim audit will be to *ascertain* and *record* the accounting and internal control systems in these areas.

Required:

Briefly describe FOUR methods you may use to ascertain the accounting system for the purchase of motorcycles.

(Total: 6 marks)

REVENUE AND RECEIVABLES

37 CAR PARKING

Your firm of accountants audits a limited liability company, with an accounting year end of 31 December 20X8, which deals in properties. Among its properties is a vacant city centre site which, owing to local planning regulations, will not be developed for at least three years. The directors of the company have decided to use the vacant site as a car park for up to 200 vehicles at any one time. Your firm has been asked to prepare a report on systems of control which would be appropriate in the operation of such a car park.

The company intends to operate the car park as follows:

Hours of business

Monday to Saturday 0600 hours to 2200 hours (site locked with exits and entrances barred between 2200 hours and 0600 hours and all day Sunday).

Charges	Length of stay	$
	up to 1 hour	0.20
	1 – 2 hours	0.40
	2 – 3 hours	0.60
	up to maximum of 16 hours	3.20
	overnight stay	2.00

Staffing

Number of attendants – four with only one attendant working at any one time on one shift either 0600–1400 or 1400–2200 hours. (Each attendant normally works four days per week, thus allowing for holidays and illness.)

Operating details

All cars to enter past one automatic barrier and machine which issues a date and time-stamped entry ticket to the car driver.

All cars to leave through one manned exit barrier after paying the attendant the correct fee.

Staff work routine

Members of staff on early shift from 0600 to 1400 hours must unlock exit and entrance and pay booth. At the beginning of either shift the member of staff must ensure:

(i)   that there are sufficient pre-numbered tickets in the ticket machine

(ii) that the correct date and time are being printed by the ticket machine

(iii) that the correct cash float ($20) is in the pay booth till.

When cars leave, duration of stay and fee are calculated and entered by the staff member on the pre-numbered ticket issued by the ticket machine. The correct fee is received by the attendant, who retains the pre-numbered ticket.

At the end of the shift all cash received should be either banked (day shift) or deposited in the night safe (night shift) by the appropriate attendant and cash float of $20 retained. The pay booth must be securely locked when the car park is closed and during any short absence of an attendant. During the afternoon a member of accounts department staff from head office collects all used tickets and records of cash banked. All accounting records are maintained at head office.

Required:

(a) Prepare an audit programme detailing two tests of control you would perform to ensure that income is complete. **(4 marks)**

(b) Explain why the tests (in (a)) will give you this assurance, i.e. completeness of income. **(2 marks)**

Note: this question is longer and more detailed than you are likely to experience in the exam, but is a good question to aid revision. **(Total: 6 marks)**

38 GREEN

In November 20X1 your firm was appointed as auditors to Green, a gardening equipment manufacturer. To assist in the planning of the audit of the company's financial statements for the year ended 31 May 20X2, the audit manager obtained knowledge about Green and the gardening equipment industry. In the course of his enquiries he was informed that the company sold only on credit terms and that it had incurred several material irrecoverable debts during the year. These had occurred due to fundamental weaknesses in the sales and trade receivables system.

Required:

Describe FIVE substantive procedures that your firm should carry out to verify the irrecoverable debts figure as reported in the financial statements of Green for the year ended 31 May 20X2. You are required to consider irrecoverable debts relating only to trading.

(Total: 10 marks)

39 LONDGLAS & CO

In May 20X2, Londglas & Co Chartered Certified Accountants were approached by the directors of Wilsun, a limited liability company, and asked to act as the company's auditors. Having carried out its normal client acceptance procedures, and having communicated with the company's previous auditors, the firm was duly appointed.

The directors of the company own all of the share capital of Wilsun. The company sells high quality television sets, digital versatile disc (DVD) players and accessories, from four retail stores located in separate towns. Each store also has a large workshop, from where large teams of engineers repair high quantities of televisions and DVD players, brought in and collected after repair, by customers. The customers pay for the repair works on collection of their property. There are also separate teams of engineers based at each store employed to install television aerials supplied by the company. All engineers are paid weekly, receiving a basic hourly rate of pay and regular high bonus payments based on a very complex productivity scheme.

The audit engagement partner in charge of the audit of the financial statements of Wilsun is Mr Cool. He is now planning the audit for the year ending 31 January 20X3 and has been informed by the directors of the company that they have received an offer from a third party to buy all of their shares in the company. The final offer price will depend upon the company's trading results for the current financial year.

In his initial planning procedures, Mr Cool assessed the inherent risk associated with the audit as being 'high'. Having ascertained and evaluated the control procedures of the company he has assessed the associated control risk as being 'low'.

FAU: FOUNDATIONS IN AUDIT

Required:

Identify FOUR significant factors that you would expect to have influenced Mr Cool to assess as 'high' the inherent risk associated with the audit of the financial statements of Wilsun. You should explain the significance of each factor identified.

(Total: 10 marks)

40 HAYDN CO

Haydn Co is a limited liability company and wholesale supplier of stationery products. It commenced trading in 20X1 and now has 60 employees with separate sales and accounts departments. However at a recent board meeting, concern was expressed at some aspects of the company's internal control, including those relating to sales and trade receivables.

Jon May, the sales director is an excellent salesman and has been largely responsible for the company's growth since 20X1 and for the implementation of the control activities exercised over the company's sales and trade receivables system. The following policies and procedures form part of the control activities exercised over that system.

1. Haydn Co uses a networked integrated sales and general ledger accounts system. The company's accountant and assistant accountant, together with Jon May and the trade receivables department clerks (sales clerks) have full access to all sales ledger files including the master file.

2. Requests from potential customers to open a credit account are forwarded to Jon May, who carries out full credit checks before deciding whether to grant a credit facility. When credit facilities are granted a sales clerk updates the sales ledger master file with the new customer details. Credit limits are not applied to customer accounts as Jon May considers this to be a restricting factor in achieving sales targets. Slow or late paying customers are pursued for payment by Jon May.

3. Customer orders received, in writing or by telephone, are directed to a sales clerk. After establishing that a trade receivables ledger account exists, the clerk uses a sales invoicing program to generate a pre-numbered sales invoice and accompanying goods despatch note addressed to customers for products as ordered. The program prices sales invoices automatically using authorised prices stored in a standing data file. Full access to this file is restricted to Jon May and the sales clerks.

4. Sales clerks post invoices as prepared to Haydn Co's trade receivables ledger, and the automated accounting system immediately updates the company's general ledger with the trade receivables ledger postings. On a daily basis:

    - all invoices are mailed by the sales clerks to customers and the goods despatch notes are forwarded to the stores department to accompany goods as and when despatched

    - a copy of each invoice is forwarded to the assistant accountant who is responsible for dealing with customers' invoice queries, the issue of sales credit notes, as he deems appropriate, and the posting of credit notes to the trade receivables ledger.

Required:

From the information provided on the sales and trade receivables system of Haydn Co:

(i)   identify FOUR weaknesses in the system

(ii) describe the implication of each weakness identified

(iii) recommend improvements to address the weakness.

You should assume that there is an adequate number of employees to implement any recommendations you make.   (Total: 15 marks)

INVENTORY AND PURCHASING

41   STARLING

Starling Co manufactures a range of vacuum cleaners. It operates from large factory premises and prepares its annual financial statements to 31 January. It has a stores area from which raw materials and parts are issued to production, and a finished goods store. In recent months the company has encountered severe difficulties in controlling its inventory resulting in losses, stopped production due to the shortage of parts and incorrect valuation of inventory.

The company has been using a system of continuous inventory checking (also known as a 'perpetual inventory system') as a means of control, but the directors recognise that the system has failed during the current year. Consequently they have agreed that company employees will carry out a physical inventory count as at 31 January 20X5, as a basis for valuing inventory for inclusion in the company's annual financial statements. The directors have also agreed to seek advice from your audit firm in connection with the introduction of a satisfactory system of continuous inventory checking to be introduced from February 20X6 and also in connection with the valuation of inventory.

Required:

Describe SIX matters that should be covered by the physical inventory count instructions to facilitate an efficient and reliable count as at 31 January 20X5.

(Total: 6 marks)

42   SMARTBUY

You are part of a team auditing the financial statements of Smartbuy, a limited liability company. The company sells home decorating and maintenance products from a large retail and warehouse unit.

From enquiries into the company's internal control systems you have ascertained the following information:

Inventory purchases

New inventory is ordered over the telephone by the company buyer. He maintains a record of telephone orders. When goods are subsequently received, the buyer has sole responsibility for checking goods received for quantity only, to his record of telephone orders. Invoices from suppliers are sent to the buyer for authorisation, before being forwarded to the Accounts Department for entry into the accounting records and subsequent payment.

FAU: FOUNDATIONS IN AUDIT

Revenue

Customers either pay by cash or cheque and the company operates electronic cash tills. Till receipts are issued to customers but till rolls are not retained. On a daily basis each till operator independently empties their till and takes the day's takings to the company cashier. The cashier counts the total daily takings and makes the appropriate entries in the company's accounting records before depositing the monies with the company's bank.

You are aware from a review of the controls exercised over the company's bank account that the cashier is responsible for reconciling the monthly bank statements to the bank account in the nominal ledger.

Required:

With regard to the inventory purchases system of Smartbuy:

(i) identify THREE deficiencies in the system

(ii) describe the implication of each deficiency identified

(iii) recommend improvements to address the deficiencies.

You should assume that there is a sufficient number of employees in the company to operate effective controls. **(Total: 15 marks)**

43 M

M, a large manufacturing company limited by liability, has all of its production, stores and head office buildings situated on a single site. The buying and accounts departments are located in the head office building.

Following a recent takeover of the company, the new directors have been informed that there is an inadequate level of internal controls over the purchases and trade payables system. Weaknesses include an absence of control procedures and adequate documentation.

The company's accounting system incorporates fully integrated purchase and general ledgers.

Required:

Describe FIVE internal controls that should exist in M over the requisitioning and authorisation of purchases.

(Total: 10 marks)

44 ZED

Zed, a large manufacturing company, conducts its operations from a single site, comprising production, stores and head office buildings. The buying and accounts departments are located in the head office building.

Following a recent takeover of the company, the new directors have been informed that there is an inadequate level of internal controls over the Purchases and Trade Payables system. Weaknesses include an absence of control procedures and adequate documentation.

The company's accounting system incorporates fully integrated purchase and general ledgers.

Required:

Identify FIVE internal controls that should exist in M over the acknowledgement of the receipt of goods and the return of goods to suppliers.

(Total: 10 marks)

PAYROLL

45 PEACH CO

Peach Co is a manufacturing company employing 190 production employees, all of whom are paid through the company's monthly wages system by bank credit transfer. The following controls are exercised over the system, with regard to the recruitment and payment of employees.

1   Potential employees are interviewed by the production manager who forwards the details of successful candidates, the job title and the rate of pay to the company's personnel manager for an employment offer to be made.

2   On receipt of acceptance of an employment offer, the personnel manager forwards written details of the employee to the wages department. A wages clerk then immediately updates the wages master file with details of the future employee, including rate of pay, standard hours of employment and the employee's bank details.

3   Employees are paid an hourly rate on the basis of time worked. In this regard the company operates a swipe card time recording system, operated by employees with individual uniquely coded swipe cards. On the first day of their employment, the production manager issues a swipe card to employees and updates the time recording unit master file with the new employee details.

4   Employees work a standard five-day week. Each day, employees register their arrival and departure by swiping their card through one of ten un-monitored entry/exit terminals. The terminals are connected to the time recording unit, which produces weekly and monthly summaries of employees' attendance records.

5   The production manager has 'amend' and 'download' remote access to the time recording unit enabling him to read recorded data via his desktop computer, amend as required and then download hard copies of the information via his desktop printer. On a weekly basis, the production manager checks the hours worked for each employee and updates the electronic data file record for each employee with any appropriate amendments, including those for holiday and sickness entitlements. The time recording unit is programmed to provide a monthly summary of hours, only after the production manager has confirmed that all the required amendments have been entered.

6   The wages manager has 'read' and 'download' remote access to the data stored in the time recording unit. On a monthly basis, he downloads hard copies of the weekly and monthly summaries to his desktop printer. He then files the summaries and passes a copy of the monthly hours summary to a wages clerk for the input of hours into, and the running of, the monthly wages programme.

FAU: FOUNDATIONS IN AUDIT

7   On completion of processing, prior to the update and closure of the programme, the following printouts are provided:

   (i)   Monthly wages summary. Showing, by employee and in total: hours paid, hourly rate, gross pay, statutory deductions, other deductions and net pay.

   (ii) Monthly bank credit transfer payments summary. Showing relevant bank account details for each employee and payments due.

   (iii) Monthly statutory deductions and other deductions summary. Showing deductions by category and payment instruction details.

8   The wages manager then scrutinises all summaries for completeness and accuracy of processing and investigates any apparent discrepancies. After satisfactory completion, a wages clerk then updates and closes the wages programme. All summaries are then filed chronologically by the wages manager, who then passes a signed approved copy of the 'bank credit' payments summary to the company's cashier. The cashier then immediately instructs the company's bank to make the relevant payments.

Required:

With regard to the wages system of Peach Co:

(i)   Identify FOUR deficiencies in the system.

(ii) Describe the implication of each deficiency identified.

(iii) Recommend improvements to address the deficiencies.

Note: You should assume that there are a sufficient number of employees at appropriate levels to operate effective controls. **(Total: 15 marks)**

46   CAFÉS

Cafés, a limited liability company, operates 30 cafés across two regions. Each region has its own regional manager responsible for all café operations and each café has its own manager. All are paid fixed monthly salaries through the head office monthly salaries system. Regional managers visit each café on a weekly basis. Due to the low rate of pay most of the cafés have a high turnover of employees. Whilst the hourly rate of pay is authorised by the board of directors, the manager of each café is responsible for their own recruitment including the completion of starters and leavers documents.

The following controls are exercised over the computer-based weekly wages system:

(i)   The wages software program includes extensive programmed input and processing controls.

(ii) The weekly payroll combines wages for both regions. Separate wages clerks based at head office are responsible for processing the wages of each region. Each clerk operates a terminal and they each have unrestricted access to all files in the wages system.

(iii) Every week each café manager prepares and authorises computer input wages time sheets showing the total hours worked by each hourly paid café employee. They also prepare starters and leavers forms, and these together with the timesheets are despatched weekly to the wages department at head office, for payment one week in arrears.

(iv) The weekly timesheets data and starters and leavers information is input into the computerised system by the wages clerk. On completion of input and processing, the system produces wages slips, which are forwarded to the company accountant for the issue of wages cheques. Once authorised, cheques together with accompanying wage slips are then handed to the wages clerks for forwarding to the café managers and distribution to employees.

(v) At the end of each payroll run, a report is printed by region and in total showing the number of employees on the system, the number of employees paid in the week and the employees' gross and net wages payments. This report is not used but it is filed with a printout of each weekly payroll. The system has facilities to produce exception and rejection reports and also detailed master file amendment and update reports, but these facilities are not used.

(vi) No other employees are involved in the procedures for the processing or authorisation of wages payments.

Required:

(a) **From the information provided identify and comment briefly on FOUR matters that would significantly affect the auditor's assessment of the level of inherent risk, applying to the wages figure as reported in the financial statements of Cafés.**

(8 marks)

(b) **Define control risk and comment briefly as to whether the auditor of Cafés should assess this risk as 'low' or 'high' when auditing the wages figure.** **(2 marks)**

(Total: 10 marks)

47 RECRUITMENT

Recruitment Co is a limited liability company which operates as a prestigious, executive recruitment agency. Its most recent financial statements are those for the year ended 31 March 20X5. The directors of the company have developed a strong control environment in the company and have introduced effective internal controls. These include the review of monthly management accounts at formal monthly board meetings and the use of a non-current assets register.

The company has 36 employees, most of whom are provided with an executive type of company car. It is company policy to purchase only new cars and to replace them when they are two years old. Employees are allowed to purchase replaced cars, and they do so by forwarding sealed bids to the company as and when replaced cars become available. To protect the company from receiving only low bids from employees, sealed bids are also received from independent motor car dealers.

During the year ended 31 March 20X5 the company purchased large quantities of office furniture, as part of an ongoing expansion programme. This included $30,000 of furniture which was ordered on 18 February 20X5 but in respect of which the company had not been invoiced by 31 March 20X5. The company's accounting records show that the furniture was delivered on 31 March 20X5 and that the associated supplier invoice was received on 31 May 20X5, some two weeks after the company's financial statements were presented for audit.

Required:

Explain why it is particularly important that there should be strong internal controls over the disposal of cars by Recruitment Co.

(Total: 6 marks)

FAU: FOUNDATIONS IN AUDIT

MANAGEMENT LETTER

48 LAKE FOUNDRY

Lake Foundry is a small limited liability company producing aluminium and copper components for local industrialists. The company uses traditional methods of manufacture and is managed by Mr W Shore and his son Mr A Shore. The ordinary share capital is owned equally by the two men and the company is at present going through a transitional stage, whereby Mr W Shore is retiring from the business and transferring the majority of his shareholding to his son. The company employs 24 people and has an annual revenue of $650,000.

The accounting records comprise a memorandum cash book, nominal ledger, receivables and payables ledgers. At present, sales orders, which are normally received on the telephone, are recorded in a two-part delivery note book only when the order has been produced and is ready for despatch to the customer. When the goods are delivered, one part of the delivery note is given to the customer and the other part remains in the book.

The sales orders are normally for small quantities of goods and because of this, the sales invoice is produced from the delivery note book at the end of each month. Mr A Shore agrees a price for the job with each customer and writes this price on the delivery note. The invoice is produced and posted to the receivables ledger by Mrs V Shore, Mr A Shore's wife, at the end of each month. Mrs V Shore is responsible for the maintenance of all accounting records other than wages, which are produced and prepared by a wages clerk.

The company costs its products in the following way:

For example:

	Job no. 123
	$
Cost of raw material	
5kg at $10 per kg	50.00
Labour, overhead and profit	
25% of raw material cost	12.50
Selling price	62.50

Mr A Shore normally purchases raw materials by telephoning the order to their suppliers. When the goods are received, Mr A Shore checks that the goods are correct as regards their quantity and type, and passes the supplier's goods received note to Mrs V Shore. When the supplier's invoice is received, it is posted immediately to the purchase ledger by Mrs V Shore. The company normally pays its suppliers at the end of the month following the receipt of the purchase invoice, which is scrutinised by Mr A Shore when signing cheques.

The company does not produce monthly management or financial information. The management is worried about the lack of growth of the company and wishes to expand the business.

You have recently been appointed as auditor of the company for the year ended 31 March 20X8 and having ascertained and tested the system of internal control, you are about to prepare the management letter.

PRACTICE QUESTIONS : SECTION 2

Required:

Prepare a management letter for Lake Foundry, incorporating in your letter deficiencies and recommendations for improvements in the internal control system of the company.

Ensure the letter refers to the following items:

(a) its purpose

(b) the level of management controls including recommendations for additional informational and organisational controls, and also the implications of the impending retirement of Mr W Shore

(c) sales and receivables

(d) purchases and payables.

(Total: 15 marks)

Note: this question is longer and more detailed than you are likely to experience in the exam, but is a good question to aid revision.

49 VENTAIR

You are the senior auditor in charge of the audit of Ventair, a limited liability company that produces air-conditioning systems to customer specifications. During the audit for the year ended 30 June 20X0 you have ascertained the following weaknesses within their systems of internal control:

- The ordering, recording and payment for purchases of materials are made by the administration department manager.

- When goods have been completed they are transferred to the finished goods area to await loading for delivery; these goods are not checked to ensure they agree with the customer order.

- All production department workers are paid on an hourly basis as per the hours on their time records; these records are completed by each worker on a weekly basis and are not checked by the supervisor prior to being submitted to payroll department.

- The office workers are paid monthly by direct transfer to their bank accounts; any changes to the salaries are notified verbally to payroll department by the personnel manager.

Required:

Based on the above information, draft the management letter to Ventair giving:

(i) a description of the deficiencies

(ii) implications of the deficiencies

(iii) recommendations to address the deficiencies.

(Total: 15 marks)

KAPLAN PUBLISHING

FAU: FOUNDATIONS IN AUDIT

EVALUATION TECHNIQUES AND TESTING

50 SHIRTS

You are in charge of the interim audit of the wages system of Shirts, a limited liability company, a manufacturer of men's clothing. The company employs 80 hourly paid staff and wages are processed weekly through a computer-based accounting system.

The following controls are exercised within the system:

(i)   a clock card system is used to record hours worked

(ii) all rates of pay and starters and leavers records are authorised by the Managing Director and notified to the Chief Accountant for updating of the wages master file

(iii) the information on the weekly clock cards is checked and summarised onto a wages data sheet by the Production Supervisor and this summary is then checked, adjusted for deductions and additions and authorised by the Production Manager. The clock cards and details of adjustments are then forwarded together with the authorised wages data sheet, to the Wages Supervisor

(iv) after checking by the Wages Supervisor, the wages data is computer processed by a Wages Clerk, the payroll is produced and then forwarded to the Chief Accountant for his review and authorisation before nominal ledger posting and payment of wages

(v)   figures including statutory and non-statutory deductions from wages are posted to the nominal ledger from the authorised payroll by the Assistant Accountant. Payment is made to each employee by way of bank credit transfer and all amounts paid are entered in the company's cash book by the Company Cashier.

Having recorded the wages system by flowchart, evaluated the controls and carried out tests of control (compliance tests) which proved satisfactory, you are now preparing to carry out substantive procedures on the wages figure shown in the interim accounts of Shirts.

Required:

Describe FIVE substantive tests that you would wish to carry out with regard to the wages figure included in the interim accounts of Shirts.

(Total: 10 marks)

CONTROLS IN COMPUTER SYSTEMS

51 KOLA

Kola, a limited liability company, is a wholesaler of toys and novelty goods. The directors, and major shareholders, are Tom and Fred Simms.

The company sells to both large and small retailers. It has approximately 750 active customers on its receivables ledger and holds as inventories a very wide range of items. It has recently purchased a desktop computer together with inventory and receivables ledger programs. These packages are now in use but, for the time being, the other accounting systems remain entirely manual.

Your firm has recently been appointed as auditor of Kola for the year ending 31 December 20X8 and the directors have invited you to visit the company's premises and acquaint yourself with the company's activities and accounting systems. They have also asked for your advice on appropriate control procedures for the computer based accounting systems.

You ascertain that the computer is a standalone system, linked to a printer. The receivables ledger and inventory packages were purchased from a small software house on the advice of Tom's friend. The latter is a sole trader who is in a similar, but smaller, line of business to Kola.

The computer is the responsibility of Anne Hughes, the cashier and bookkeeper who has worked for Kola for one year. Anne is assisted in the office by two accounts clerks.

The computer is kept on Anne's desk. She tells you that the hard disk is backed up to a writeable CD every Friday. The backup CD is kept in her office drawer next to the locked petty cash box.

As you discuss the system with Anne, Fred Simms enters her office and opens an account for a new customer. You note that the password, an 8-digit number, is taped to the monitor screen. No printout of this transaction is obtained. He has also just received a large cheque from a customer and he posts it on to the receivables ledger as he wishes to bank it immediately. He leaves a note of the customer and cheque amount on Anne's desk so that she can enter it into the manual cash book later in the day.

Anne confirms that anyone in the office can use the computer as it is there to reduce her workload. She admits that the control accounts do not always balance, but she presumes that this is something 'the auditors can sort out at the year end'.

The warehouse supervisor updates the computerised inventory records daily after Anne has finished work for the day. Tom Simms informs you that the supervisor carries out monthly test counts, agreeing physical inventory to inventory records. He has not been informed by the supervisor that there are any problems. He tells you that he doesn't see why you can't reduce your audit work as you can rely on the accuracy of the computer.

Required:

Write a letter to Tom Simms explaining why audit planning is especially important where small desktop computer based accounting systems are involved; highlight your explanations by using examples from Kola.

(Total: 10 marks)

52 OILCO

You are the auditor of Oilco, a limited liability company, a major petroleum refiner, and you are about to commence the interim audit. The company utilises a computerised accounting system operated by a central computer with on-line terminals located in several departments. Many computer input documents remain paper-based whilst customers of Oilco require hard-copy invoices for their records. The audit senior has asked you to take charge of the interim audit of revenue and receivables, and has arranged a meeting between yourself and the accountant responsible for the receivables section.

Required:

List SIX questions to ask the accountant at the scheduled meeting to enable you to make an initial evaluation of the effectiveness of the computer controls over revenue and receivables.

(Total: 6 marks)

FAU: FOUNDATIONS IN AUDIT

53 SOMETECH

Sometech, a limited liability company of which you have always been the auditor, has operated a computer-based accounting system since its formation in 20X2. The next set of accounts to be audited are those for the year ended 30 September 20X9, and it is now 1 December 20X8.

The directors have recognised the need to consider the introduction of an improved computer-based accounting system and the development of a new system is about to commence.

As the company's auditor you will be consulted throughout the development process. Further, the directors appreciate that once the new system has been accepted as operational and run live, you will be particularly concerned to ensure the continued existence of application controls and effective general controls (including controls to prevent unauthorised amendments to data files).

Live running of the new computer based accounting system is planned to commence on 1 September 20X9 and for a four-month period running up to that date, it is intended that the existing system and the new system should be run alongside each other. The directors of the company have asked what effect this plan will have on your audit of the company's accounts for the year ended 30 September 20X9.

Required:

(a) In the context of a computer based accounting system, explain what you understand by each of the following terms:

    (i) application controls (2 marks)

    (ii) general controls. (2 marks)

(b) Explain why Sometech should run both the existing and new systems alongside each other prior to live running of the new system and give the reasons why you, as company auditor, would wish to be involved at this stage of the development process of the new computer based accounting system. (6 marks)

(Total: 10 marks)

54 SEMI

Semi is a small limited liability company owned and controlled by the Popsi family. It operates as an importer and distributor of wines, purchasing from suppliers in various countries and distributing to wholesale and high street retail outlets. Mr Popsi is the Managing Director of the company and the other two directors of the company are members of his family.

The company employs only five clerical staff, all working in the same office, comprising two sales clerks, two buying clerks and a relatively inexperienced bookkeeper. The bookkeeper reports directly to Mr Popsi, neither have received any formal accountancy training.

The company's existing accounting system is only partially automated, by way of a computer-based receivables ledger system operated by the bookkeeper. The only management information Mr Popsi receives from the bookkeeper is monthly sales summaries. Mr Popsi has identified the need to improve the quality of accounting information and to speed up the processing of accounting transactions within the company.

Consequently, having taken advice from a business acquaintance, he has decided that the company will implement a small computer-based accounting system using a standard 'off the shelf' accounting software package, with fully integrated ledgers, loaded onto a Personal (desktop) Computer. The system will be operated solely by the bookkeeper.

Mr Popsi is unaware of the control problems likely to exist in the transfer of current data to the small computer-based accounting system and the subsequent operation of the system. He has therefore asked you for guidance on these issues.

Required:

(a) **Briefly comment on whether the quality of management information and the speed of processing of accounting transactions within Semi is likely to improve, following the installation of a small computer-based accounting system.** **(4 marks)**

(b) **Identify SIX potential areas of concern in the transferring of data to, and the subsequent use of, the computer-based accounting system.** **(6 marks)**

(Total: 10 marks)

55 FOZZ

Fozz, a limited liability company, manufactures microwavable convenience foods.

Your firm's audit partner has been told by the directors that the company is about to develop a new, on-line computer-based accounting system. They have stated that they will require the company's auditors to give guidance on the controls to be exercised over the development of the new system.

Required:

Describe the effect that the existence of the new computer-based accounting system will have on the planning of the audit of the financial statements of Fozz.

(Total: 6 marks)

AUDIT EVIDENCE (INCLUDING COMPUTER-BASED SYSTEMS) AND SAMPLING

GENERAL PRINCIPLES

56 AUDIT EVIDENCE I

The examination of evidence is fundamental to the audit process. Standard auditing practice requires that auditors should obtain relevant and reliable audit evidence sufficient to enable them to draw reasonable conclusions therefrom. Evidence is available to the auditor from sources under his own control, from the management of the company and from third parties. Each of these sources presents the auditor with differing considerations as to the quality of the evidence so produced.

Required:

(a) Discuss the quality of the following types of audit evidence, giving two examples of each form of evidence:

    (i) evidence originated by the auditor (2 marks)

    (ii) evidence created by third parties (2 marks)

    (iii) evidence created by the management of the client. (2 marks)

(b) Describe the general considerations which the auditor must bear in mind when evaluating audit evidence. (4 marks)

(Total: 10 marks)

57 AUDIT EVIDENCE II

You are to be involved in the forthcoming audit of the accounts of a toy manufacturing company and junior colleagues in your team have asked you to provide them with explanatory notes on the concept of audit evidence. They are aware that 'computation' is an example of a procedure used by the auditor to obtain audit evidence, however they have asked that the notes contain details on other procedures to be employed to obtain audit evidence on the forthcoming audit.

Required:

Prepare notes in any format for the colleagues in your team which:

(a) define the term 'audit evidence' (2 marks)

(b) identify and explain TWO limitations or constraints that are placed upon the auditor when collecting audit evidence (2 marks)

(c) identify TWO procedures (in addition to 'computation') which the audit team will use when gathering evidence on the audit of the accounts of the toy manufacturing company. (2 marks)

(Total: 6 marks)

58 AUDIT EVIDENCE III

An auditor may obtain audit evidence by one or more of the following procedures:

1 Inspection

2 Observation

3 Recalculation

4 Analytical procedures.

Required:

Explain what each of these procedures involves.

(Total: 6 marks)

PRACTICE QUESTIONS : SECTION 2

59 AUDIT EVIDENCE IV

For each of the procedures identified below which are used to obtain audit evidence, describe what it involves and provide an example of its use:

(i)   Observation; and

(ii) Recalculation.

(Total: 6 marks)

60 EMPLOYMENT AS A JUNIOR AUDITOR

You have been short-listed along with one other applicant for employment as a junior auditor with a local firm of Chartered Certified Accountants. They have asked you both to attend a final interview at which you will each give a presentation on audit evidence.

Your presentation must include comment on:

(i)   financial statement assertions

(ii) procedures used by auditors to obtain audit evidence.

Required:

List and describe THREE procedures other than enquiry and confirmation that an auditor might use to obtain audit evidence.

(Total: 6 marks)

INVENTORY

61 DIAMOND

It is recommended that where inventories are a material item the auditor should attend the inventory count. Your client Diamond, a limited liability company, is a jeweller, and has two shops both located in busy cities 20 kilometres apart; all inventories are held at the two premises and the control of the inventories is performed by staff at each shop location. You have attended the inventory count to confirm the accuracy of the inventory quantities and you are now working on inventory valuation.

Prior to commencement of the audit, the managing director informed you that there have been recent price wars in the industry and therefore some of the inventory has had to be valued at its net realisable value (NRV).

Required:

List THREE tests that you could perform at the year end to ensure that the net realisable value of the inventory valuation is correct.

(Total: 6 marks)

KAPLAN PUBLISHING

62 EMERALD

Auditors would normally attend the inventory count when the inventory valuation is a material item. Your client Emerald, a limited liability company is a jeweller, and has four shops sited in town centre locations within 30 kilometres of each other; inventories are held at all four locations and control of the inventories is performed by staff at each of the shops. On occasion, inventories have been transferred between two of the locations due to inventory shortages and the transfer was recorded at both locations. Prior to commencement of the audit, the managing director informed you that there have been recent price wars in the industry and therefore some of the inventory had to be valued at its net realisable value (NRV).

Required:

List the main reasons for the auditor's attendance at the inventory count, and state whether you would attend the inventory count at all, or just some, of Emerald's shops with the reasons for this decision.

(Total: 6 marks)

63 COACHES

Coaches, a limited liability company, operates a fleet of 150 coaches (or buses) for private hire. It employs a maintenance team of mechanics and fitters working continuously on ongoing and emergency maintenance. Consequently the company keeps a large inventory of spare maintenance parts for issue to maintenance jobs. Many of the parts are high value items.

The parts inventory is housed in stores adjacent to the maintenance workshop, and is controlled by a stores supervisor and his assistant using a very basic computerised inventory recording system, to which only these two staff and the financial director of the company have access. The stores supervisor and his assistant have received no formal training in using the system.

The system identifies each inventory line by a part number, part description and location. It can be updated for quantity movements only and allows for reference to goods received notes (receipts into inventory) or maintenance job cards and goods returned notes (issues out of inventory). All goods received notes, maintenance job cards and goods returned notes are pre-numbered.

The computerised inventory records are not independently checked during the year, therefore the financial director of Coaches has issued instructions for a year-end inventory count, which is to take place immediately after the close of business on the last day of the financial year. You have received a copy of the instructions for review.

Required:

(i) **Explain your reasons for giving particular audit attention to goods received notes, maintenance job cards and goods returned notes issued both immediately before and immediately after the year-end inventory count.**

(ii) **Identify audit procedures you would carry out in connection with these documents.**

(Total: 10 marks)

PRACTICE QUESTIONS : SECTION 2

64 SWEET SCENTS

Sweet Scents Co is a wholesale supplier of cosmetic, beauty and perfumery products. The company's inventories are stored in a central warehouse and a computerised system, updated from goods received notes and goods despatched notes, identifies quantities of inventories held by product number and description. Inventories are counted only at the company's year-end date.

In discussions with the auditors about their forthcoming audit of the company's financial statements for the year ending 30 June 20X5, Sweet Scents Co's financial director made the following statements:

1   'Our employees will carry out a thorough count and valuation of all inventories as at 30 June 20X5. However, because employees of your firm will be in attendance at the count and will check inventory values, your firm will be responsible for the accuracy of the reported inventories figure.'

2   'Most of the company's inventories are stored in sealed cardboard boxes, as delivered to the company, which are labelled with product descriptions, quantities and use-by dates. This will make inventories easy to identify and easy to count.'

3   'On 31 May 20X5 a flood at the warehouse caused varying degrees of damage to some of the inventories. The damaged inventories were not covered by insurance but as we will be valuing them at cost they will not be separately identified at the inventory count on 30 June 20X5.'

4   'Approximately five per cent of the value of our inventories is represented by Fleurs Bleu perfumery products. These were purchased in July 20X4 in anticipation of a high demand, but due to a public health scare we haven't sold any. We are resigned to the fact that these products are worthless but we'll wait until the next financial year before we throw them out and write them off.'

Required:

(a)   **Comment on the validity of statement (1) of the financial director as to the audit firm's responsibility for the accuracy of the inventories figure at 30 June 20X5.**

(2 marks)

(b)   **With reference to each of the statements (2), (3) and (4) made by the financial director to the auditors of Sweet Scents Co:**

(i)   **identify and explain the concerns the auditors should have with regard to the accuracy of the inventories figure to be reported in the company's financial statements for the year ending 30 June 20X5; and**

(ii)   **state the action the company should take both at the inventory count and in the valuation process to overcome these concerns.**

(Note: Parts (i) and (ii) above carry equal marks.)   (13 marks)

(Total: 15 marks)

65 JEANS

Jeans, a limited liability company, manufactures high fashion jeans for distribution to wholesalers and retailers.

You have been assigned to the audit of inventory in the company's financial statements for the year ended 31 July 20X3.

The following points are relevant to the audit:

(i) The company has raw materials, consumables and work in progress inventory at its factory base. Finished goods are stored in a separate warehouse located five kilometres away. The company does not hold inventory owned by third parties.

(ii) On 31 July 20X3 employees of the company will physically count the inventory at both of the company's sites and members of your audit team will be in attendance.

(iii) The company has significant quantities of finished goods inventory held by independent retail stores under its sale or return system. Under this system, inventory is displayed for sale at retail shop premises but remains the property of Jeans until it is sold by retailers. Any garments not sold within three months are returned to Jeans for bulk sale at heavily discounted prices.

(iv) Some quantities of finished goods inventory were stated at net realisable value in the financial statements of the company for the previous year.

Required:

(i) **Define inherent risk.** **(2 marks)**

(ii) **Explain why the inherent risk associated with inventory in the financial statements of Jeans would be assessed as 'high'.** **(8 marks)**

(Total: 10 marks)

NON-CURRENT ASSETS

66 ANDREW MANUFACTURING

Your firm has recently been appointed auditor of Andrew Manufacturing, a limited liability company, and you have been asked to carry out the audit of non-current assets at the company's year-end of 30 September 20X4.

The company operates from its own freehold premises, and the draft accounts show the following movement on non-current assets for the year.

	Freehold property $	Plant and machinery $	Motor vehicles $	Total $
Cost:				
At 1 October 20X3	162,577	46,003	20,175	228,755
Additions	2,534	8,721	7,500	18,755
Disposals	–	(5,937)	(5,250)	(11,187)
At 30 September 20X4	165,111	48,787	22,425	236,323
Depreciation:				
At 1 October 20X3	2,104	20,059	10,353	32,516
Charge for the year	1,102	4,878	5,741	11,721
On disposals	–	(4,808)	(3,937)	(8,745)
At 30 September 20X4	3,206	20,129	12,157	35,492

It is the company's policy to charge a full year's depreciation in the year of acquisition and nothing in the year of disposal.

The company's accounting policies are to provide depreciation at the following rates:

Buildings	4% on cost
Plant and machinery	10% on cost
Motor vehicles	25% on cost

The company maintains a non-current asset register for plant and machinery and motor vehicles.

Required:

Prepare an audit programme detailing the tests you would perform for the audit of non-current assets for the year ended 30 September 20X4.

(Total: 15 marks)

RECEIVABLES

67 ASKWITH

You are a senior audit clerk and are briefing an inexperienced junior auditor who is about to commence the audit of the receivables of Askwith, a limited liability company. The receivables ledger is maintained by the client on a mainframe computer. Sales invoice and credit note data are fed to the computer via 12 terminals in regional offices. All cash entries, journal entries relating to irrecoverable debts and other adjustments, and any other special entries are input via two terminals located at the client's head office. The computer produces, as a monthly routine, an aged receivables schedule containing on average 3,000 live balances. You tell the junior auditor to verify the accuracy of the aged receivables schedule including arranging for circulars to be sent to a representative sample of receivables. To assist the junior in this task you provide him with a copy of the audit programme.

The audit programme contains, among other things, the following:

(a) For balances over $1,000 at the year-end, use special computer audit program to dump transaction details for one month prior to the year-end and for one month after the year-end.

(b) Circularise receivables (seeking a positive response) and follow up those who do not reply.

(c) Test cut-off using dumped transactions.

The new junior audit clerk is still a little confused by some of the terminology being used, the reasons underlying your requests and the detail of the techniques being used, and has asked you for further assistance and information.

Required:

(a) **Explain to the junior auditor the steps that should be taken if no reply is received from the relevant customers and explain what alternative procedures might be used to verify the balances.** **(5 marks)**

(b) **Prepare an audit programme for the audit of the financial statements for the year ended 30 June X8 detailing the cut off tests that should be used to verify that the cut off for receivables is correct.** **(10 marks)**

(Total: 15 marks)

FAU: FOUNDATIONS IN AUDIT

CASH

68   BON VOYAGE

You are the partner in charge of the audit of Bon Voyage, a limited liability company, which runs a travel agency business through a head office in London and ten retail shops spread throughout the country, six of which have been opened during the last year. A medium-term bank loan was negotiated to cover the additional working capital required for this expansion.

Extracts from the summarised statements of financial position as at the year ends of 30 November 20X5 and 20X4 are as follows:

	20X5		20X4	
	$	$	$	$
Tangible assets*:				
Non-current assets		163,000		199,000
Current assets:				
Trade receivables and prepayments	197,500		141,400	
Bank	37,600		41,200	
Cash (floats, unbanked cash, travellers' cheques)	67,000		52,500	
	302,100		235,100	
Liabilities:				
Trade payables, customers deposits and sundry accruals	166,200		146,400	
Net current assets		135,900		88,700
Total assets less current liabilities		298,900		287,700
Liabilities: amounts falling due after more than one year:				
Bank loan		60,000		–
		238,900		287,700

*   A tangible non-current asset is one that physically exists and can be touched.

As partner in charge of the audit you are concerned as to the extent and quality of the audit work performed by your firm.

Required:

Prepare a working paper to form part of the planning section of the current audit file providing guidance to the auditors who will be conducting the work stating the evidence required for the following items in the statement of financial position:

- **bank and bank loans**
- **cash (floats, unbanked cash and travellers' cheques).**

(Total: 10 marks)

PRACTICE QUESTIONS : SECTION 2

LIABILITIES AND OTHER ITEMS

69 PEAR CO

Pear Co is a long established building renovations company and prepares its annual financial statements to 30 April. The financial statements for the year ended 30 April 20X8 revealed the following item, together with comparative for the previous year.

Item	30 April 20X8 $	30 April 20X7 $
Trade payables	315,000	205,200

Pear Co's reported pre-tax profit for the year ended 30 April 20X8 was $990,000.

Required:

List FIVE substantive procedures that the auditor of Pear Co should carry out to verify the completeness and valuation assertions for trade payables.

(Total: 10 marks)

70 APPLE CO

Apple Co is a long established building renovations company and prepares its annual financial statements to 30 April. The financial statements for the year ended 30 April 20X8 revealed the following item, together with comparative for the previous year.

Item	30 April 20X8 $	30 April 20X7 $
Provision	81,000	–

The provision of $81,000 relates to a legal obligation to carry out repairs to a public building damaged by employees of Apple when renovating an adjoining building. Apple Co's reported pre-tax profit for the year ended 30 April 20X8 was $990,000.

Required:

List FIVE substantive procedures that the auditor of Apple Co should carry out to verify the completeness and valuation assertions of the provision balance.

(Total: 10 marks)

71 FARRINGTON

You are the manager in charge of the audit of Farrington, a limited liability company, which manufactures biscuits and confectionery. You wish to instruct a junior member of staff to audit the trade payables, accruals and provisions as shown in the statement of financial position at the year-end and are in the process of preparing audit programmes which clearly explain the purpose and extent of the work at each stage of the audit.

FAU: FOUNDATIONS IN AUDIT

The draft figures as at 31 October 20X5 (with 20X4 comparative figures) are as follows:

	31 October	
	20X5	20X4
	$	$
Trade payables	261,521	177,625
Sundry accruals	21,162	18,177
Provisions:		
Legal action*	40,000	–
Factory repairs**	72,000	62,000
	394,683	257,802

*   This provision relates to a legal action brought by a competitor who claims that their manufacturing process has been illegally copied.

** This provision, which was first set up in 20X4, relates to sums required to be spent on urgent repairs to the factory foundations and structural steelwork. ($58,500 was spent during the year ended 31 October 20X5).

Required:

Prepare an audit programme detailing the tests to be performed to verify the figure for Trade Payables. **(6 marks)**

72 OXTON WHOLESALERS

Auditors carry out certain procedures during their audit work to ensure that assets are not overstated and liabilities are not understated in the statement of financial position.

You are the audit senior carrying out the audit (year end 31/12/X5) of Oxton Electrical Wholesalers, a limited liability company, who sell electrical products to retail stores. They sell both major home entertainment appliances such as audio systems, home cinema kits and televisions, and consumables such as tapes and disks. All of their purchases are made on credit; terms are usually 30 days. The draft figure in the financial statements for payables is twice the amount as at last year, yet revenue has remained constant.

Required:

Describe audit procedures to be performed to ensure that trade payables and accruals are not understated as at the yearend 31/12/X5. **(10 marks)**

73 CLOTHING

Clothing is a limited liability company engaged as a wholesaler of clothing, purchasing into inventory from numerous suppliers on credit terms. As an Audit Senior, you are about to commence detailed testing on the trade payables figure reported in the company's accounts for the year ended 31 March 20X0.

The company operates a computer-based accounting system, incorporating fully integrated payables and nominal ledgers, and following an initial review you concluded that the system should meet its designated objectives.

Tests of control on the internal control measures existent in the system, including application and general controls with regard to the computer-based accounting system, proved to be satisfactory.

Required:

Identify FIVE substantive procedures that you would wish to carry out when verifying the trade payables figure in the accounts of Clothing for the year ended 31 March 20X0.

(Total: 10 marks)

SAMPLING

74 AUDIT SAMPLING

Explain the following terms as applied to audit sampling methods.

(i)	Haphazard selection; and	(3 marks)
(ii)	Systematic selection.	(3 marks)

(Total: 6 marks)

75 CROMWELL

Cromwell, a limited liability company, sells fashion accessories through approximately 500 shops and has a head office in Andover.

Each shop operates an imprest system and holds a cash float of $250 to provide change for the till and to cover sundry expenses. All cash takings are banked at the end of each working day.

You are the senior in charge of the audit and your manager has indicated that only a sample of the cash balances held by the shops will be the subject of audit tests.

Many of the fashion accessories are purchased from foreign suppliers and the company's buyers frequently travel abroad. The cashier at head office therefore holds a substantial amount of foreign currency in her safe.

The company has recently expanded its accessory range and prior to year end received a bank loan of $500,000 repayable over three years.

The cash balance at year end 31 March 20X7 totalled $100,000.

Required:

Prepare a general working paper explaining the main factors which will be taken into account when determining the sample size for substantive testing. This will be used to assist the other members of the audit team helping you with the testing.

(Total: 10 marks)

FAU: FOUNDATIONS IN AUDIT

AUDIT COMPLETION

76 REVIEW AND REPORTING

Review procedures form an important part of the audit process and audit firms may employ more than one method of review. Review types include:

1 'Hot' Reviews

2 'Cold' Reviews.

Required:

For each of the review types listed above, state when and by whom it should be carried out and state what should be gained from a thorough review.

(Total: 6 marks)

77 AUDITORS' OPINION

Describe TWO of the four differing circumstances in which it is appropriate for auditors to modify their audit opinion on a company's financial statements. Your answer should state the type of opinion that should be expressed in each circumstance.

(Total: 6 marks)

78 GOING CONCERN

Your firm has selected you to attend a discussion workshop as part of your audit training programme. Attendees at the workshop will discuss the auditor's responsibilities in the audit of financial statements regarding the appropriateness of the going concern assumption as a basis for the preparation of the financial statements.

Required:

State FIVE audit procedures to obtain evidence that the going concern assumption is appropriate for an entity.

(Total: 10 marks)

79 TOBY

The annual financial statements of Toby, a limited liability company, were prepared to 31 March 20X1.

In December 20X0 the company's auditors read a newspaper report that the company was about to announce employee redundancies. The report raised doubts about the future of Toby.

In January 20X1 the auditors commenced their initial planning procedures for their audit of the Toby's annual financial statements. Their work included a preliminary assessment of the risk that Toby would be unable to continue as a going concern.

Having now almost completed their audit of the annual financial statements, the auditors have concluded that there is a significant level of concern about Toby's ability to continue as a going concern.

Required:

Identify THREE financial indicators and THREE non-financial indicators that may have led the auditors to conclude that there was a significant level of concern about Toby's ability to continue as a going concern as at 31 March 20X1.

(Total: 6 marks)

80 GOING CONCERN CONCEPT

Auditors must consider the going concern concept as part of their work on behalf of clients.

Required:

(a) Explain what is meant by the going concern concept, and describe the effect that this concept has on the preparation of financial statements. **(4 marks)**

(b) state two situations when the going concern concept is not to be used in the preparation of financial statements. **(2 marks)**

(Total: 6 marks)

81 LAMBLEY PROPERTIES

You are the manager in charge of the audit of Lambley Properties, a limited liability company, and you have been asked to prepare the letter of representation which will be signed by the company's directors.

You are aware that there are two material items in the accounts for the year ended 31 January 20X3 on which you want the company's directors to confirm that the treatment in the accounts is correct:

(a) One of the company's subsidiaries, Keyworth Builders, is experiencing going concern problems, and you want the directors' confirmation that they intend to support the company for the foreseeable future.

(b) Eastwood Manufacturing is in dispute with Lambley Properties over repairs required to a building they purchased from Lambley. Lambley Properties constructed the building for Eastwood, and three years after it was sold to Eastwood, the customer is claiming that repairs are required which will cost $3 million, and that Lambley is liable to pay for these repairs, as they are as a result of negligent construction of the building. In addition, Eastwood is claiming $2 million for the cost of disruption of its business due to the faults in the building and in the period when the repairs take place. Lambley Properties has not included any provision in its accounts for this claim. Lambley Properties have obtained the advice of a lawyer and a surveyor, and the directors believe there are no grounds for the claim and any court action will find in their favour. However, Lambley Properties has included a note in its accounts concerning this contingency.

Required:

(a) Explain to the junior auditor assisting you with the work the reliability of a written representation letter as audit evidence and the extent to which an auditor can rely on this evidence. **(5 marks)**

(b) Prepare an audit programme detailing FIVE procedures you would perform to check whether a provision should be included in the accounts for the legal claim from Eastwood Manufacturing. **(10 marks)**

(Total: 15 marks)

FAU: FOUNDATIONS IN AUDIT

AUDIT REPORT

82   JONES, ROBERTS, WILLIAMS

You are currently engaged in reviewing the working papers of several audit assignments (all limited liability companies) recently carried out by your audit practice. Each of the audit assignments is nearing completion, but certain matters have recently come to light which may affect your audit opinion on each of the assignments. In each case the year end of the company is 30 September 20X8.

(a)   **Jones** (Profit before tax $150,000)

On 3 October 20X8 a letter was received informing the company that a trade receivable, who owed the company $30,000 as at the year end had been declared bankrupt on 30 September. At the time of the audit it was expected that creditors ranking as unsecured liabilities (such as Jones), would receive nothing. The directors refuse to change the accounts to provide for the loss, on the grounds that the notification was not received by the year end date.

Total debts shown in the statement of financial position amounted to $700,000.

(b)   **Roberts** (Profit before tax $500,000)

On 31 July 20X8 a customer sued the company for personal damages arising from an unexpected defect in one of its products. Shortly before the year end the company made an out-of-court settlement with the customer of $10,000, although this agreement is not reflected in the financial statements as at 30 September 20X8. Further, the matter subsequently became known to the press and was extensively reported. The company's legal advisers have now informed you that further claims have been received following the publicity, although they are unable to place a figure on the potential liability arising from such claims which have not yet been received. The company had referred to the claims in a note to the financial statements stating, however, that no provision had been made to cover them because the claims were not expected to be material.

(c)   **Williams** (Net loss for the year $75,000)

Three directors of this manufacturing company owed amounts totalling $50,000 at the end of the financial year, and you have ascertained that such loans were not of a type permissible under company law. These amounts had been included in the statement of financial position with other items under the heading 'Receivables'. The directors did not wish to disclose these loans separately in the accounts, even if such disclosure is required by law, as they were repaid shortly after the year end, as soon as they were made aware that the loans were not permissible. The directors have argued that the disclosures could prove embarrassing and that no purpose would be served by revealing this information in the accounts.

Required:

Prepare a memorandum addressed to the other partners in the firm, to include:

(i)   a discussion of the problems in each case

(ii)   reference to materiality considerations

(iii) relevant accounting principles and appropriate accounting standards (where appropriate), and

(iv) an indication, with reasons, the kind of audit report (including the type of qualification, if necessary) which you consider would be appropriate in each case.

You are not required to produce the full audit reports, and you may assume that all matters other than those specifically mentioned are considered satisfactory.

Note: this question is longer and more detailed than you are likely to experience in the exam, but is a good question to aid revision. **(Total: 15 marks)**

83 TAGGART

You are one of the audit partners in a firm of accountants and are currently dealing with the audits of two of your clients, all of which are limited liability companies. It is January 20X8 and you have just returned from a meeting with the other partners and your secretary has given you messages from each of the clients with details of actions they propose to take; these actions have a bearing on the audit and are as follows:

(a) Taggart are brandy distillers and normally hold inventory for six years before selling it. During the accounting year, a large quantity of two-year-old inventory has been sold to Cloves, a merchant bank, at cost plus 5% profit. The company's normal selling price is cost plus 50%. Taggart has an option to buy back the brandy in four years' time at a price which represents the original sale price plus interest at the current market rate. The inventory has remained on the premises of Taggart, but has been recorded as a sale in their financial statements for the year ended 31 May 20X8.

(b) The directors of Wolfworld decided to incorporate a revaluation of all of its non-current assets into its financial records for the year ended 31 May 20X8. The existing policy of depreciating assets on a reducing balance basis is to be continued but the total depreciation charge for each category of assets will be divided between the amount based on historical cost and the additional amount arising as a result of the revaluation. The latter amount is to be charged against the revaluation reserve leaving only the historical cost charge to be charged against profits.

Required:

Write letters to the directors of each of the two companies i.e. Taggart and Wolfworld, explaining the audit implications of each of the situations.

Indicate in the letters the reasons why there is an audit problem and suggest solutions which would ensure the truth and fairness of the financial statements.

(Total: 15 marks)

84 B CO

B Co is a recently formed limited liability company and has a forecast annual revenue of $5 million.

The directors of B Co wish to appoint external auditors. However, they have only a limited knowledge of matters relevant to the external audit process.

As the accountant of B Co, the directors have asked you to write a memorandum to them clarifying specific audit matters.

Required:

Explain the factors that auditors should consider in determining whether the financial statements of a company show a 'true and fair view'.

(Total: 6 marks)

FAU: FOUNDATIONS IN AUDIT

85 GEE

Gee is a recently formed limited liability company and has a forecast annual revenue of $5 million.

The directors of the company wish to appoint external auditors. However, they have only a limited knowledge of matters relevant to the external audit process.

As the company's accountant the directors have asked you to write a memorandum to them clarifying specific audit matters.

Required:

Explain what is meant by a qualified audit report opinion and the circumstances in which an auditor should express a qualified opinion on the financial statements of a company.

(Total: 6 marks)

86 BUTCAR AND COMPANY

Butcar and Company are the auditors of Colain, a limited liability textile manufacturing company.

The following points were relevant to the audit of the company's financial statements for the year ended 31 August 20X2.

- In compiling the opinion section of their report the auditors commenced with the words, 'In our opinion....', and then went on to express an unqualified opinion on the financial statements.
- Butcar and Company made extensive use of analytical procedures during the course of their audit work. The audit engagement partner considered that these had been crucial to the efficient performance of the audit.

Required:

(a) Describe the circumstances in which an audit firm should express an unmodified opinion in its report on the financial statements of a company. **(2 marks)**

(b) (i) Briefly explain the meaning of the term 'analytical procedures'. **(3 marks)**

    (ii) Explain how Butcar and Company should have used analytical procedures at:
- the planning stage **(5 marks)**
- the final overall review stage **(5 marks)**

to assist them in their audit of the financial statements of Colain for the year ended 31 August 20X2.

(Total: 15 marks)

87 TYPES OF AUDIT OPINION

When an auditor concludes that the financial statements of a company give a true and fair view, in accordance with the identified financial reporting framework, then he should express an unmodified opinion in his auditor's report on those financial statements.

Required:

Describe the circumstances in which each of the following should be expressed in an auditor's report.

(i) disclaimer of opinion **(3 marks)**

(ii) adverse opinion. **(3 marks)**

(Total: 6 marks)

Section 3

ANSWERS TO MULTIPLE-CHOICE QUESTIONS

THE BUSINESS ENVIRONMENT

1 D

The objective of an audit is 'to enable the auditor to express an opinion whether the financial statements are prepared, in all **material** respects, in accordance with an identified financial reporting framework'.

2 A

Not all companies are required to have their financial statements audited. If the UK is used as an example, small companies are normally exempt from the audit requirement. The external auditor reports on whether the published financial statements give a true and fair view, not whether they are correct or not.

THE AUDIT FRAMEWORK

3 D

4 C

5 D

These are management responsibilities, not auditor responsibilities.

6 D

Definitions as follows:

Error – 'an unintentional mistake' and could include accidental misapplication of accounting policies, oversights or misinterpretation of the facts.

Fraud –'an intentional act involving the use of deception to obtain an unjust or illegal advantage'.

FAU: FOUNDATIONS IN AUDIT

7 D

Management are primarily responsible for the prevention and detection of fraud and are responsible for implementing an effective system of internal control. The external auditors are responsible for giving an opinion on whether the financial statements are true and fair.

8 B

9 A

10 C

The business operating from a single location should lead you to consider this a *lower* risk assignment than average.

11 A

An accountant should be straightforward and honest in performing professional work, and with all professional and business relationships. Scenarios B-D describe behaviour without integrity.

12 B

A self-interest threat arises when the receipt of fees from a client represents a large proportion of the total gross fees of the audit practice as a whole. The Auditing Practices Board states that for a listed company, fees should not exceed 10% of the audit firm's annual fee income and 15% for a non-listed business. A self-interest threat will also arise as a result of the auditor accepting valuable gifts, such as a Rolex, from a client.

13 B

When accepting additional work from audit clients, separate teams can be used to reduce self-review risk.

14 C

15 D

It is fundamental that information is not made available to the new auditor without the permission of the client.

16 A

17 B

Management must design appropriate controls to reduce the risk of fraud. It is important to remember that the auditor usually has no specific statutory duty to detect fraud. However, if a material fraud affects the truth and fairness of the financial statements then this should be detected by audit work; the auditor has a duty to design procedures to give reasonable assurance of detecting material misstatements whether caused by fraud or error.

ANSWERS TO MULTIPLE-CHOICE QUESTIONS : SECTION 3

18 B

19 A

The duties of an internal auditor include objectively reviewing an organisation's business processes, evaluating the effectiveness of risk management procedures that are currently in place, protecting against fraud and theft of the organisation's assets, ensuring that the organisation is complying with relevant laws and statutes and making recommendations on how to improve internal controls and governance processes.

20 D

AUDIT PLANNING AND RISK

21 B

Materiality is not just a purely financial concern. Some items may be material by nature, regardless of size.

22 C

The audit opinion is considered at the completion stage, not at the planning stage of the audit.

23 A

Detailed testing is carried out at the evidence gathering stage, not at the planning stage of the audit.

24 A

The audit plan details the audit procedures to be carried out to put the audit strategy into effect.

25 D

26 B

Detection risk can be controlled by the auditor by e.g. varying sample sizes.

27 B

Risks 2, 3, 4, 6 and 7 are control risks. Risks 8 and 9 are detection risks.

28 B

Audit risk is made up of inherent and detection risk, but also control risk.

29 C

The auditor can manipulate detection risk in various ways, e.g. allocating complex or risky areas of the engagement to suitably experienced and competent staff, by placing more, or less, reliance on the results of systems and controls testing, by altering the volume of balances tested by changing sample sizes and by consulting external experts on technically complex or contentious matters etc.

30 A

31 D

32 D

Option D is a strength of analytical procedures, not a limitation.

33 D

Working papers are an internal source of information, produced by the audit team.

34 D

Inherent and control risks cannot be influenced by the auditor.

35 D

36 B

Option A describes detection risk. Option C describes control risk. Option D describes the risk that a fraud/error has made its way into the financial statements.

37 C

Option A describes detection risk. Option B describes inherent risk. Option D describes the risk that a fraud/error has made its way into the financial statements.

38 A

Option B describes inherent risk. Option C describes control risk. Option D describes the risk that a fraud/error has made its way into the financial statements.

39 B

Working papers may be prepared electronically e.g. on word processing or spreadsheet packages, with adequate backup.

ANSWERS TO MULTIPLE-CHOICE QUESTIONS : **SECTION 3**

40 D

Working papers may contain e.g. summaries of the results of tests undertaken, and not necessarily every detail of an assignment. Their form and content will vary between assignments. Working papers must demonstrate that sufficient appropriate evidence has been obtained during the course of the audit but some may be more narrative based, whereas others perhaps more diagrammatical.

41 D

Documents A, B and C will be held on the current file.

42 B

INTERNAL CONTROL

43 B

44 D

Segregation of duties: assigning the responsibility for recording transactions, authorising transactions and maintaining custody of assets to different employees to prevent the risk of fraud and error.

45 A

A range check is an example of an application control, not a general control.

46 B

With a test of controls, the auditor is interested in whether a control has operated correctly – the size of the transaction is irrelevant.

47 C

A walk-through test is a procedure used during an audit of an entity's accounting system to gauge its reliability. A walk-though test traces a transaction step-by-step through the accounting system from its inception to where it might appear in the financial statements.

48 D

The auditors will prepare audit programmes containing the detailed tests to be performed to achieve the audit objectives.

49 B

50 B

51 C

Tests of control – audit work performed to generate evidence as to whether the controls are operating.

52 B

Sales being made monthly is not a control objective.

53 C

Internal Control Questionnaire (ICQ) – a list of controls given to the client to say whether or not those controls are in place.

Internal Control Evaluation Questionnaire (ICE) – the client is asked what controls they have in place for a given control objective.

54 D

Payments being made through cheques only is not a control objective.

55 D

56 B

57 B

It is not the auditor's responsibility to participate in management decision making to ensure that the internal controls prevent and detect fraud and misstatements. Management are ultimately responsible for the internal controls. Auditors need to gain an understanding of the systems and controls. This enables the auditor to assess the level of control risk and to determine the audit approach to take.

58 D

59 A

Quality checks will ensure that sub-standard goods are not dispatched to customers. They will not minimise the risk of non-payment by customers.

60 D

The control environment includes the governance and management functions and the attitudes, awareness and actions of those charged with governance and management concerning the entity's internal control and its importance in the entity.

61 B

ANSWERS TO MULTIPLE-CHOICE QUESTIONS : SECTION 3

62 D

Money received being recorded and banked will reduce the risk of theft. Fulfilling all orders correctly will reduce the risk of customers receiving incorrect/ late items. Credit notes only being raised for valid reasons will reduce the risk of credit notes being issued fraudulently.

63 A

64 B

Carrying out credit checks for all customers will reduce the risk of non-payment by customers. An arithmetic check on invoices will reduce the risk of issuing an invoice for an incorrect amount. Authorisation of credit notes will reduce the risk of credit notes being raised inaccurately and for invalid reasons.

65 A

Credit limits applied being adhered to will reduce the risk of non-payment. Credit notes being matched to original invoices will reduce the risk of credit notes being raised inaccurately. An open order file, which is regularly checked, will reduce the risk of unfulfilled orders.

66 A

67 B

68 B

Control objectives are the objectives that the internal controls are seeking to achieve. Statement 2 is describing control activities.

69 A

The action described in Statement 3 will reduce the risk of an invoice being paid twice.

70 C

71 A

The goods arrival area being kept secure will reduce the risk of theft of good received. Managers authorisation being required before orders placed will reduce the risk of purchases being made for invalid business reasons. Purchase invoices being matched to the goods received notes will reduce the risk of incorrect orders being accepted.

72 B

73 C

In order to check whether supplier statements have been reconciled monthly, the auditor could take the top 10 suppliers, obtain supplier statement reconciliations, ensure evidence of review, re-perform and follow up discrepancies.

FAU: FOUNDATIONS IN AUDIT

74 D

In order to check whether authorisation has been obtained for new suppliers, the auditor could obtain list of new suppliers added to payables ledger and check appropriate authorisation is in place.

75 C

76 B

77 D

78 A

A test of control involves the auditor obtaining evidence that the client has implemented the controls they say they have, and that they have worked effectively, during the period.

79 D

The five components of internal controls in accordance with ISA 315 are the control environment, monitoring of controls, information system, control activities and the entity's risk assessment process.

80 D

Effective controls increase the chances of fraud detection – this is a strength, not a limitation.

81 B

82 D

Analytical procedures MUST be carried out at the planning stage and the review stage of an audit and may also be used during the evidence gathering stage. They would not be used after the audit report has been issued in order to confirm the validity of the audit opinion.

83 B

The PRIMARY purpose of an auditor evaluating and testing the internal controls is to test the effectiveness of the control used by the client to prevent or detect material misstatements. Depending on the results of these tests, auditors may choose to rely upon a client's system of controls as part of their auditing activities.

AUDIT EVIDENCE (INCLUDING COMPUTER-BASED SYSTEMS) AND SAMPLING

84 D

Accuracy, valuation and allocation – assets, liabilities and equity interests have been included in the financial statements at appropriate amounts and any resulting valuation or allocation adjustments have been appropriately recorded, and related disclosures have been appropriately measured and described.

85 A

Completeness – all transactions and events that should have been recorded have been recorded, and all related disclosures that should have been included have been included.

86 D

Inspecting evidence of ownership will test rights and obligations, not existence.

87 A

88 C

The most reliable form of evidence is auditor generated evidence (A and D). The next most reliable is third party generated evidence (B) and the least reliable is client generated evidence e.g. a written representation letter.

89 D

A confirmation letter cannot be used as confirmation of inventory held at the client as more reliable evidence can be obtained by the auditor by way of an inventory count.

90 C

Written evidence is more reliable than oral evidence. Independent external evidence is more reliable than internally generated evidence.

91 C

92 C

Systematic selection – where a constant sampling interval is used (e.g. every 50th balance) and the first item is selected randomly.

FAU: FOUNDATIONS IN AUDIT

93 A

When a positive receivables circularisation is used, the recipient should reply whether or not they are in agreement with the balance. It is more effective than a negative receivables circularisation whereby only those disagreeing with the balance should reply. The circularisation of receivables satisfies a number of objectives: (i) reliable evidence is provided as to whether receivables are overstated – customers can usually be relied on to complain if the balance they are supposed to owe is too large (ii) evidence, albeit weaker, is provided as to whether receivables are understated – customers are less likely to complain if the balance is too small (iii) indirect evidence is generated of the accuracy of the sales figures.

94 C

Statement 1 – if sales volumes have decreased, this is inconsistent with an increased sales value. *Statement 2* – if purchases increase, the cost of sales figure will also increase, leading to a lower gross profit figure. This could adequately explain the decrease in the gross profit percentage. *Statement 3* – discounts received are shown as 'income' below the gross profit in the income statement, meaning that statement 3 will not affect the gross profit percentage.

95 A

96 D

97 C

Existence cannot be tested through NRV tests. NRV tests will provide assurance over inventory valuation.

98 D

99 D

The calculation for receivables days involves the sales figure, rather than the purchases figure.

100 D

101 B

Review of the timesheets of the warehouse staff will not provide suitable evidence for inventory and work-in-progress. Review of timesheets can be used to test the veracity of the payroll figures.

102 B

103 C

ANSWERS TO MULTIPLE-CHOICE QUESTIONS : **SECTION 3**

104 C

Statement 1 is incorrect. Auditors primarily test debit entries (assets and expenses) for overstatement and credit entries (liabilities and income) for understatement. Testing for understatement tests completeness. Testing for overstatement tests valuation, existence, rights and obligations, and occurrence.

105 B

Statement 1 is incorrect. Inventory is included in the financial statements at the *lower* of cost and NRV.

106 B

Inventory is overvalued – the net realisable value is likely to be lower than the cost of these items.

107 C

108 B

Where client has counted inventory, auditor *cannot* assume values are correct. The auditor must gather their own evidence in respect of inventory.

109 D

110 C

111 A

Bank confirmation letters are a *strong* source of audit evidence as they are generated by a third party. Petty cash need not always be counted as it is usually a small immaterial balance making it one of the least risky areas of the audit.

112 B

Greatest risk with liabilities is *understatement*. All suppliers do *not* send supplier statements on a regular basis. In order to carry out a supplier statement reconciliation you will also need access to the accounts payable ledger.

113 C

Testing rights and obligations will be appropriate for balances on the statement of financial position.

114 A

115 D

FAU: FOUNDATIONS IN AUDIT

116 C

Audit software is used to interrogate a client's system. The main advantage of these programs is that they can be used to scrutinise large volumes of data, which it would be inefficient to do manually. The procedures can simplify the auditor's task by selecting samples for testing, identifying risk areas and by performing certain substantive procedures.

117 C

Application controls relate to data integrity and ensure that only valid data is being processed and is being processed completely and accurately. Examples include batch controls, encryption, data input controls etc. but do not include administration and structure of the information system.

118 D

Test data involves the auditor submitting 'dummy' data into the client's system to ensure that the system correctly processes it and that it prevents or detects and corrects misstatements. The objective of this is to test the operation of application controls within the system. To be successful test data should include both data with errors built into it and data without errors. Data may be processed during a normal operational cycle ('live' test data) or during a special run at a point in time outside the normal operational cycle ('dead' test data).

119 D

120 C

The results of the testing of that sample can be extrapolated across the population to establish the effect of the misstatement across the population to assess whether the projected misstatement is greater than tolerable misstatement.

($42/$2,500) * $10,000 = $168

The projected error of $168 is greater than the tolerable misstatement of $75. Further audit work is required for this population.

121 C

122 D

123 B

A sales invoice being omitted would lead to the receivables balance being *understated*, rather than overstated.

ANSWERS TO MULTIPLE-CHOICE QUESTIONS : SECTION 3

AUDIT COMPLETION

124 A

Due to issues over breaching confidentiality, one firm of auditors would not review the working papers of another firm.

125 C

A fire in a warehouse in the week immediately after the reporting date which destroyed the company's inventory is normally a non-adjusting event. Statement 2, however, says that ALL the company's inventory was destroyed. If a non-adjusting event impacts the going concern assumption, the event becomes an adjusting event as the going concern basis of preparation may no longer be appropriate.

126 D

127 A

128 D

129 D

130 A

It is not the auditor's responsibility to determine whether, or not, an entity can prepare its financial statements under the going concern presumption; this is the responsibility of management. The auditor's responsibility under ISA 570 is to obtain sufficient appropriate audit evidence about the appropriateness of management's use of the going concern assumption in the preparation of the financial statements, and to conclude whether there is a material uncertainty about the entity's ability to continue as a going concern.

131 D

132 B

Non-adjusting events are indicative of a condition that arose after the end of the reporting period and do not result in adjustment to the financial statements. They should be disclosed if of such importance that non-disclosure would affect the ability of the users to make proper evaluations and decisions.

133 C

134 B

135 B

A disclaimer of opinion is issued when a limitation on scope is imposed by the client and, as a result, the auditor is unable to obtain sufficient appropriate audit evidence.

136 C

137 A

A qualified opinion would be most appropriate, stating that the financial statements of the client are fairly presented, except for a specified issue.

138 B

An adverse opinion would be most appropriate, indicating that the company's financial statements are misrepresented, misstated and do not accurately reflect its financial performance and health.

139 C

An emphasis of matter paragraph included in the auditor's report refers to a matter appropriately presented or disclosed in the financial statements that, in the auditor's judgment, is of such importance that it is fundamental to users' understanding of the financial statements. The inclusion of the paragraph should not affect the auditor's opinion on the financial statements.

Section 4

ANSWERS TO PRACTICE QUESTIONS

THE BUSINESS ENVIRONMENT

1 ADVANTAGES OF AUDIT

>
>
> **Key answer tips**
>
> In each section a short paragraph is written on each point. This breaks the answer up, and is much easier to mark, as well as improving presentation. The examiner does not want to see a long wordy essay.
>
> The main advantage common to all forms of audit is that the accounts have been subjected to an independent review and an independent and professional opinion obtained on their truth and fairness.
>
> Incidental advantages are the detection of irregularities, the moral deterrent against fraud and error, and the availability of expert technical advice on such matters as the improvement of systems, taxation and accountancy. More specifically, the advantages depend on the types of audit.

(a) (i) Companies

In the case of companies, shareholders must of necessity place great reliance upon a review of the accounts by an independent qualified auditor since they do not have access to the books and records of the company and they are not always familiar with the businesses in which they have an interest, nor indeed with the accounting practices adopted.

Moreover, the audit ensures that the directors have fulfilled their statutory obligations, and acts as a precaution against fraud on the part of employees.

Additional benefits deriving include the improvement of the company's control and information systems, and possibly advice on improvement in standards of the company's reporting to its members (shareholders).

(ii) Partnerships

Audited accounts in the case of a partnership provide a reliable basis for the division of profits and for the settling of accounts between partners, reducing the possibility of disputes and facilitating their settlement should they arise.

Audited accounts will assist in settling the partnership tax assessments and provide a basis for negotiation in the case of an incoming partner or the sale of the business.

On the death of a partner the total amount due to his estate should be more readily determined and agreed, and the settlement of death duties facilitated.

The provision of reliable audited accounts presents a more acceptable basis for the negotiations involved in raising additional finance.

In the special situation of a firm which has 'sleeping' partners, an audit is of particular importance and advantage as such persons take no part in the management of the business.

(iii) Sole traders

Similar advantages accrue to the business of a sole trader, since there is a possibility of a breakdown in internal control and accounting systems.

An incidental but important advantage of an audit is that the professional firm of accountants acting as auditors will be available to provide other services e.g. advice and assistance on accounting, costing, management, taxation and systems problems.

(b) Limitations of external audit in relation to fraud

An auditor conducting an audit in accordance with International Standards on Auditing (ISAs) is responsible for obtaining reasonable assurance that the financial statements taken as a whole are free from material misstatement whether caused by fraud or error. Owing to the inherent limitations of an audit there is an unavoidable risk that some material misstatements of the financial statements may not be detected even though the audit is properly planned and performed in accordance with ISAs.

It is commonly believed that the purpose of the external audit is to detect, and report, fraud and error. The detection and reporting of such matters is secondary to forming an opinion on the financial statements.

Material fraud is often very difficult to detect, however, and an auditor has not necessarily failed in his duty if he fails to detect such a fraud.

Most frauds are small, and immaterial to the financial statements. If auditors detect frauds, they have a duty to report such matters to the management of the company regardless of whether they are material or immaterial. Only matters that are material need to be reported in the financial statements.

2 X CO

Report on the auditor's duty to detect fraud

Prepared by: Auditor

Date:

Terms of reference

To produce a report on the auditor's duty to detect fraud for the Finance Director of X Co.

Responsibility to detect fraud

The primary responsibility for the prevention and detection of fraud rests with management. The auditor's responsibility is limited to designing and evaluating his work with a view to having a reasonable expectation of detecting those irregularities which might impair the truth and fairness of the view given by the financial statements.

X's situation

In the case of X Co, the auditor has a duty to form an opinion as to whether inventories are fairly presented i.e. the inventories are correctly owned, valued and disclosed. Auditors should obtain sufficient, relevant and reliable evidence to support their opinion, and should carry out their work with due skill and care.

The auditors of X Co planned their attendance at branch inventory counts and attended the main warehouse inventory count. The work carried out by the auditors would appear, on the basis of the information given, to be adequate, assuming that it was carried out expeditiously. In the absence of further details, conclusions as to whether or not the audit was properly carried out cannot be drawn.

3 LIMITATION OF LIABILITY OF AUDITORS

Key answer tips

A difficult question requiring a lot of knowledge about auditor's liability. When discussing alternatives and commenting on various proposals from the question it is always appropriate to bring in relevant information and practical points. Do not though give impractical or irrelevant advice; this will not be highly marked.

(a) An auditor's liability could be limited by:

(i) limiting the maximum amount of any one claim; or

(ii) limiting the number of claims made by one individual against the auditor over a given amount of time.

The first system has been proposed at various times, although rarely actually used and is, in fact, currently unlawful in some countries. This could be a very practicable way of limiting liability as long as the potential individuals who could make any claim could be identified. Too many claims i.e. from each and every shareholder would then not be allowed, or allowed to a percentage of the total limit. When the limit was set, potentially by statute to avoid protracted disagreement between shareholders and auditors, then it would be easy to enforce and give auditors the benefit of lower insurance premiums.

The second system has additional problems in that again the persons who must claim can be identified, but also now the time period for claims must be agreed, and also any sliding scale limiting the amount of claims should two or more be made during the time period, whatever it is. This would tend to make the whole claiming process very arbitrary and thus unworkable.

In practice, therefore, only the first system would work, and this would require statutory backing to ensure that it was fair to all parties concerned.

(b) (i) An investor may look to the auditor to redress him for any losses incurred as a result of an incorrectly produced audit report. If the auditor is to enjoy some extent of limited liability then the investors' potential claim will be limited. It is therefore very likely that investors would not consider some limitation of auditor liability acceptable, as they may not then receive back the full amount of their loss.

(ii) An auditor must always perform sufficient work to ensure that his audit procedures identify all material errors in the financial statements to a given level of risk. Thus, most auditing firms ensure that to a risk level of 5% they have identified all material errors. All material errors therefore should have been found although potentially 5 errors out of 100 will have been missed.

Setting an upper limit to potential claims does not in itself affect the level of materiality, although the auditor's perception of risk may change. Auditing would become less risky because the amount of claims is smaller. An auditor may therefore feel justified in decreasing the amount of work actually done to meet the lower level of risk. This will further mean that costs are decreased on an audit as fewer items will be tested. This cost benefit can then either be passed onto the client in lower fees or increase the return to the auditing firm.

Less audit work being done though must increase the likelihood of a material error in the financial statements. Fewer items are tested and therefore fewer errors will be found.

In conclusion, setting an upper limit to liability claims may have the dual effect of decreasing perceived audit risk, but increasing the actual risk of a material error in the financial statements. The audit opinion will therefore be less reliable.

(c) (i) It will normally be practicable to limit an auditor's liability as long as:

1 the upper limit of the claim can be agreed between the auditor, company and shareholders; and

2 members accept the higher amount of risk involved regarding the lack of identification of material errors.

In practice the upper limit may well be a percentage of shareholders' funds on the statement of financial position, although for very large clients this will still result in extremely large upper limits to claims.

(ii) The reliability of the audit opinion will be affected in two ways:

1 With less work being done the auditor is likely not to find so many errors in the accounts. This will decrease the reliability of the audit opinion as fewer problems are expected to be found and reported on to the members.

2 Because the auditor does accept an upper limit for his liability, members will correctly or otherwise perceive that the audit opinion is less reliable. The auditor is no longer accepting full liability and so personal assets are safer; it is therefore likely that less work will be done as the same amount of work is no longer necessary.

(iii) Although auditors' liability could be limited, it would not appear to be the best course of action because:

1 Members' and the public's confidence in auditors will be decreased by the implication that less work will be done and therefore the audit opinion devalued.

2 The setting up of a fair and just system would be difficult.

3 In particularly large claims where the auditor is at fault, the system would work against the member who could not recoup his losses from the auditor.

In conclusion, I believe that auditors' liability should not be limited.

4 EXTERNAL AUDITORS

(a) External auditor independence

(i) External auditors are required to provide an independent assessment of the truth and fairness of a company's financial statements, and are therefore unable to fulfil their duties to shareholders if they are not independent of the entity on which they are reporting.

(ii) If external auditors have an interest in the financial statements on which they are reporting, they may not be objective. For example, if, in the case of a listed company, they have prepared the financial statements on which they are reporting, their view may not be considered objective.

(iii) If they have financial or employment connections with the company on which they are reporting they will not be objective.

(iv) If they provide a significant level of additional services to the entity, some argue that they cannot report objectively as auditors to shareholders.

(b) Advantages and disadvantages of external auditors providing consulting services

The principal advantage of providing consulting services lies in the fact that auditors are best placed to provide such services, because they have an intimate knowledge of the operations of the company.

Equally, if they provide consulting services, the knowledge so obtained will be useful in conducting the audit, and experience in general of consulting better enables auditors to conduct their duties as auditors, because knowledge of other industries can be brought to bear on the client.

The principal disadvantage is that, as auditors often make a lot of money from non-audit work, their objectivity in these circumstances is impaired, due to an unwillingness to challenge directors or issue a qualified audit report for fear of losing lucrative consulting work.

Another disadvantage is that if the auditors have implemented the systems that produce the financial statements, they are unlikely to give a qualified audit report on the information that those systems produce.

5 EXTERNAL AUDITOR RESPONSIBILITIES

Responsibilities of external auditors to directors and shareholders

(i) The external auditors are required to prepare a report to shareholders on the truth and fairness (or fair presentation) of financial statements prepared by management for the benefit of shareholders as a group.

(ii) The auditors, if appointed by shareholders, act as agents for the shareholders in the same way as directors act as agents for the company.

(iii) Auditors have no specific duties to directors (other than the contractual relationship) although it is clearly necessary that an adequate working relationship is formed in order that the audit can be performed properly. Directors generally have a duty to provide auditors with the information and explanations they require to perform the audit.

(iv) Auditing standards require that auditors report weaknesses in systems that they discover during the course of their audit to management ISA 260 *Communication with those charged with governance* (ISA 260).

(v) Auditors will normally report fraud to the directors except where director involvement is suspected. Fraud will also be reported to the appropriate authorities.

FAU: FOUNDATIONS IN AUDIT

THE AUDIT FRAMEWORK

6 EAGLE CO

(i) 'Audit sampling' is the application of audit procedures to less than 100% of the items within an account balance or class of transaction (a population) to enable the auditor to obtain and evaluate audit evidence about some characteristic of the item selected in order to form, or assist in forming, a conclusion concerning the population.

(ii) The advantages of using statistical sampling rather than judgemental sampling (non-statistical sampling) include:

1. The size of the sample is determined objectively having regard to the degree of risk associated with the area being tested.

2. Bias is eliminated.

3. Results of statistical sampling can be more easily justified as being representative of the population as a whole, thus increasing the level of confidence in the results of testing the sample. As a consequence of this, the conclusion drawn from the results of sample testing are more easily justified where an audit client disputes the audit conclusions.

4. The emphasis on risk assessment by the auditor in the determination of the sample size encourages the auditor to concentrate on significant issues (for example a high degree of control risk), which may not otherwise be considered.

5. In instances when there is a large population, the use of statistical sampling techniques may reduce the sample size, and therefore the amount of audit work required, as compared to the sample size that would be selected using judgement sampling methodology.

6. The auditor may justifiably conclude with a definite level of confidence that the conclusions drawn from the sampling test is within stated precision limits.

7 SPARROW CO

Examples of the working papers ordinarily contained in a typical current audit file include:

- evidence of the planning process including audit programmes and any changes thereto
- evidence of the auditor's consideration of the work of internal audit department and conclusions reached
- analyses of transactions and balances
- analyses of significant ratios and trends
- the identified and assessed risks of material misstatements at the financial statement and assertion level
- a record of the nature, timing and extent of audit procedures performed in response to risks at the assertion level and the results of such procedures
- evidence that the work performed by assistants was supervised and reviewed
- an indication as to who performed the audit procedures and when they were performed
- details of audit procedures applied regarding components whose financial statements are audited by another auditor

- copies of communications with other auditors, experts and other third parties
- copies of letters or notes concerning audit matters communicated to or discussed with management or those charged with governance, including the terms of the engagement and material weaknesses in internal control
- letters of representation received from the entity
- conclusions reached by the auditor concerning significant aspects of the audit, including how exceptions and unusual matters, if any, disclosed by the auditor's procedures were resolved or treated
- copies of the current year's financial statements and auditor's report.

8 ETHICS

(a) Exceptions to the principle of retaining confidentiality of clients business and financial affairs:

- Where the client has given specific authorisation for disclosure to be made. Ideally, this authorisation should be obtained in writing to avoid any misunderstanding between the auditor and the client.
- Where there is a legal duty to make disclosure. In the UK, an example of this would be if the auditor had reasonable grounds for believing that the client was involved with money laundering activities.
- Where there is a public duty to make disclosure, which is not usually clearly defined or explained in law. An example of this could be where the auditor becomes aware that there is a significant risk to the health and safety of the general public. This may arise, for example, if the auditor becomes aware that a client has not complied with relevant law which then poses a danger to the public, such as the client dumping toxic waste near to a reservoir.
- Where the auditor is required to give evidence in court under oath. In such circumstances, the auditor must comply with the legal requirements imposed upon him.

(b) Mechanisms a firm could adopt to ensure good ethical practices include:

- Appointment of an 'ethics champion' or ethics partner within the firm.
- Conducting a formal independence review prior to acceptance of any audit appointment.
- Implement regular training and communication of policies and practices for staff on ethical issues.
- Rotation of audit appointment partner and staff to ensure that undue familiarity of the client does not develop and that objectivity is maintained.
- Monitoring of fee levels to ensure that the firm does not rely unduly upon the income from one client.

(c) Explanation of the advocacy threat:

In order to maintain objectivity and independence, auditors should not take on a management or decision-making role on behalf of a client. When an auditor provides audit, advisory or consultancy services to a client, there is a clear risk that they may take on a management or decision-making function on behalf of a client.

When an auditor undertakes advisory services on behalf of a client, they should ensure that they provide advice only and that any decision-making is done by the client. For example, an auditor may be asked to provide advice or consultancy services to a client in relation to the acquisition of another company, a takeover.

However, it should be the client's decision as to whether or not they acquire another company and on what terms and conditions they are willing to do so.

It would not be appropriate for an auditor to adopt a decision-making role on behalf of a client. This would impair their independence and objectivity and consequently undermine the credibility of the audit function. Care should therefore be exercised that, when providing advice to a client, there are sufficient controls in place to minimise the risk of making decisions on behalf of clients.

9 FASTBIKES

Briefing Notes – Auditor appointment and eligibility	
Criteria	External auditor
Eligibility to act	To be eligible to act as an external auditor membership of an RSB (Recognised Supervisory Body) is required. Examples of RSBs are the ACCA and ICAEW, and the individual or firm must be eligible for appointment under the rules of that body.
Security of tenure	The external auditor has a contract with the client which is detailed in the engagement letter. Appointment of an auditor is dictated by legislation, and is usually for the period from one AGM to the next. The members' rights of removal are also contained within the legislation. In such cases the auditor has the right to make written/verbal representations in respect of his removal. Management may also have the right to 'dismiss' the auditor. The auditor's rights of resignation are dictated by law.
Primary objective	The key objective of the external auditor's work is to report to the members on the truth and fairness of the organisation's financial statements.
Limitations on scope of work in order to achieve the objective(s)	There are no limitations on the scope of the external auditor's work. The external auditor has a responsibility to obtain sufficient information and explanations necessary to provide him with evidence to be able to form an opinion on the truth and fairness of the financial statements (which is his primary objective – see point above).

10 SUJON

(a) The control environment can be seen as part of the culture of a company. It encompasses the general attitudes of management and staff to control systems and their level of awareness of the importance of sound controls and operating procedures to the success of the organisation.

A strong control environment is one where control systems are given a high level of relevance and importance. Such a control environment would be characterised by the involvement of experienced managers committed to the implementation and operation of sound control procedures. The managers and staff involved should operate within an appropriate organisation structure with clearly defined lines of authority and responsibility.

There should be a positive attitude to the training, development and motivation of employees who are encouraged to identify possible improvements in existing control systems.

(b) If the external audit function is to retain its credibility, it is important that the auditor should be independent of the company under audit. In this context, rules of professional conduct established by ACCA warn auditors of areas of activity where their independence may be drawn into question. One such 'danger' area is the situation where the auditor becomes involved in the management of the company or participates in taking management decisions on behalf of the company.

As far as the audit partner attending the Board meeting is concerned, consideration needs to be given as to the reason for the attendance and the role which the auditor is likely to play at the meeting.

In the case in question, if the role played by the audit partner is purely an advisory one (for example explaining the benefits which the company may gain from establishing an internal audit department), independence is unlikely to be impaired. If this is the case, it would be advisable for the auditor to make it clear to the Board in advance that he is attending purely as an advisor.

Where independence may be seen to be jeopardised is if the audit firm is expected to become involved in selecting the staff to be employed by the company in the internal audit department. Whereas involvement in the earlier stages of the recruitment and selection process may well be acceptable, the final decision on who should be appointed is a decision for management – the auditor should make it clear that the firm cannot be involved in this decision.

11 RESPONSIBILITIES REGARDING FRAUD

The external auditor might discover fraud by chance while gathering evidence about the truth and fairness of the financial statements. The external auditor would only look for fraud if there were some reason to believe that it might have affected the truth and fairness of the financial statements.

However, the external auditor is expected to identify material fraud, except in situations where the fraud was well hidden.

The external auditor will report fraud (material or otherwise) to management (as long as management themselves are not involved in the fraud) and again to the appropriate authorities as part of their compliance with money laundering requirements in most countries.

12 AUDIT PROGRAMMES

Standard audit programmes	
Advantages	**Disadvantages**
Standard programmes ensure that all possible relevant audit areas are covered	A standardised approach may lead to complacency in evaluating whether specific audit procedures are relevant for a specific audit client
Standard programmes can help to reduce training time and costs	Standard programmes may lead to work being done without members of the audit team fully understanding what they are doing and why, only that they are repeating what was done in a previous audit

Advantages	Disadvantages
Standard programmes may help to improve understanding and application of the work and quality control procedures required by the firm	Standard programmes may result in work not being done when it is required simply because it is not included in the standard programme
Standard programmes could still be subject to customisation for each client by adding additional relevant tests or identifying and explaining why specific tests are not required as part of the audit or a specific client	Customisation or amendment may be undertaken by a less experienced member of the audit team or may be done without proper supporting explanation or documentation

13 INDEPENDENCE PROBLEMS

Key answer tips

It is quite common for questions to ask for a description or explanation of something and then to apply that same concept to a practical matter. Independence is a complicated issue because it raises questions about whether the auditor is independent and those may have very little to do with whether the auditor appears to be independent. This could mean that different answers could gain full marks provided a realistic case is made.

Auditors are required to report their unbiased opinion on the truth and fairness of the financial statements. The auditor's personal interests, such as a desire to retain an appointment or a sense of personal loyalty to the company whose accounts are being audited, should not distort that opinion. Professional objectivity is an attitude of mind that enables the auditor to gather sufficient evidence to form a valid opinion and to report honestly on whether the financial statements give a true and fair view even if the directors attempt to discourage such honesty.

The statement suggests that it does not matter whether auditors appear to lack objectivity provided they are objective. Such a situation could arise if the users of the audit report have an unfounded belief that the auditor's opinion could have been biased. They could, for example, believe that the auditor would not report honestly because a substantial fee is being paid for the audit. It is true that the auditor's actual objectivity is of paramount importance in terms of how the auditor behaves. The audit report will not reassure the users, though, unless they believe that the auditor is actually independent. If the auditor does not appear to be independent, the audit report will not enable the shareholders to rely on the financial statements and the audit will have been largely pointless.

Auditors must also appear to be independent or they will discredit the accountancy profession. Professional people should be seen to behave in an honest manner, otherwise their qualifications and associations will be devalued.

14 VISWA

(a) Duties of auditors:

- To report whether the financial statements show a true and fair view and have been properly prepared in accordance with relevant legislation.
- To consider whether information issued with the financial statements, which has not been subject to audit, is consistent with the audited financial statements.
- To make disclosures required by law if not already included in the financial statements, such as information on directors' emoluments and loans to company officers.
- To form an opinion, and make relevant disclosure if required, on additional matters that may be required by relevant legislation; UK examples include whether proper accounting records have been maintained and whether all information and explanation required from company officers has been received.
- To make a 'statement of circumstances' when ceasing to hold office for any reason.

Duties of directors:

- To safeguard the assets of the company.
- To maintain proper accounting records; in particular, there should be records of cash receipts and payments, together with details of assets and liabilities.
- To prepare annual financial statements that show a true and fair view.
- To prevent and detect fraud.

(b) Factors to consider – Reliance on work performed by internal audit

The following important criteria will be considered by the external auditors when determining if the work of internal auditors is likely to be adequate.

Extent to which its objectivity is supported

The auditor must consider the extent to which the internal audit function's objectivity is supported by its organisational status, relevant policies and procedures. Considerations include to whom internal audit reports, any conflicting responsibilities, any constraints or restrictions, whether those charged with governance oversee employment decisions regarding internal auditors and whether management acts on recommendations made.

Level of technical competence

The auditor must consider whether internal auditors are members of relevant professional bodies, have adequate technical training and proficiency and whether there are established policies for hiring and training.

Whether a systematic and disciplined approach is taken

The auditor must also consider whether internal audit activities are systematically and properly planned, supervised, reviewed and documented; and whether suitable audit manuals, work programs and internal audit documentation exist. The auditor must also consider whether the function has appropriate quality control procedures in place.

15 AUDIT WORKING PAPERS

(i) In the case of continuing audit engagements, two types of audit files are usually maintained – a permanent audit file and a current audit file.

The permanent audit file contains information of 'on-going' significance, which will be of relevance to each year's audit. The file should be updated for each audit.

The current audit file contains information relating primarily to the period currently under audit.

(ii) Examples of matters that should be recorded on the permanent file include:

- information concerning the legal and organisational structure of the company, including its principal activities, principal locations and key employees;
- important legal documents, agreements and minutes;
- information concerning the industry, economic environment and legislative environment within which the company operates;
- a description of the company's accounting systems and internal controls.

Tutorial note

The requirement for this part of the question asks for four matters, which may be found in each type of audit file. In addition to those listed above, the following items will normally be found on the permanent audit file.

- copies of final signed financial statements of the company;
- engagement details including a copy of the engagement letter, details of special audit requirements and other services to be provided by the firm;
- the history of key analytical review ratios.

Examples of matters that should be recorded on the current audit file include:

- evidence of the planning process and any 'updates';
- evidence of risk assessments and any subsequent revisions;
- a record of the nature, timing and extent of audit procedures performed, the results of such procedures and the conclusions reached;
- copies of communications with other auditors, banks, lawyers and other experts and other third parties.

Other valid examples include the following:

- letters of representation from the company's directors;
- summary of the significant aspects of the audit, highlighting audit concerns, the directors' views and conclusions reached;
- audit completion and disclosure checklist.

16 P AND PARTNERS

(a) It is important for an audit firm to have good quality control procedures across its range of activities for the following reasons:

(i) to ensure all procedures are efficiently performed thus maximising the firm's profits;

(ii) to minimise any customer complaints and any subsequent loss of business;

(iii) to ensure that no major errors are made which could result in litigation.

(b) It is important that an audit firm prepares audit working papers to provide documentary evidence of the tests and procedures that they performed in order to arrive at their audit opinion. The working papers need to be complete and sufficiently detailed for the following reasons:

(i) In the event that legal action was taken against the auditor for negligence in the completion of the audit it is important that the working papers are sufficiently detailed such that the auditor could challenge such a claim on the basis that he performed the work satisfactorily and in accordance with best practice.

(ii) Audit files need to be reviewed prior to completion of the audit and the audit opinion being agreed. In order for a reviewer to understand exactly what work has taken place and relate the conclusions to the work performed it is essential that all work is documented including any necessary explanations and consequences of results, especially where the review performed is a cold review i.e. performed once the work is completed.

(iii) Audit files can be used for 'training' or reference purposes. For example junior auditors may find it useful to read through past files to help reinforce and understand how files are structured. It is also useful for future audits of the same company to refer to the previous year's audit files especially where there were problems or points raised which needed to be resolved in future. It is also helpful to have detailed files to assist in ensuring all high risk areas are considered in future.

(iv) Having detailed files ensures that even when audit staff are not the same on subsequent audits of the same firm the knowledge obtained during the audit is not lost. In this respect it is also important that a standardised approach is adopted to facilitate ease of understanding of all aspects of the audit.

AUDIT PLANNING AND RISK

17 FINCH CO

(a) Inherent risk is the susceptibility of a financial statement assertion to a misstatement which could be material, individually or where aggregated with other misstatements, assuming that there were no related internal controls.

(b) The factors that would affect the initial assessment of the inherent risk include:

(i) the geographic spread of the hotels operated by the company. The fact that each hotel has several income streams, in addition to accommodation and meals, combined with obvious expenditure requirements represents an inherent risk with regard to income and expenditure misstatement. The risk is increased significantly due to the distance of each hotel from the head office and accounts department of Finch Co.

(ii) the existence of cash sales. Cash is a desirable and portable asset with high inherent risk of loss due to the possibility of misappropriation by dishonest individuals.

(iii) the appointment of a new unqualified financial director, with only limited hotel sector experience, during the year. This could impair the preparation of the financial statements of the company due to the adoption of incorrect accounting policies or the existence of material errors in the financial statements.

(iv) the combination of an experienced and aggressive managing director with a potentially weak financial director. This could lead to undue pressure and influence being placed upon the financial director, by the managing director, to treat items incorrectly in the financial statements or not to include them in order to falsely represent the financial status of the company, and hence improve bonuses.

(v) the existence of profit related bonuses in the remuneration packages of the company's directors and hotel general managers. This could lead individuals to overstate income, understate expenditure, or both, in order to increase reported profits for personal gain.

(vi) the construction of a new hotel during the year. Such a project would involve significant levels of expenditure by the company. Inherent risk would centre on the correct disclosures in the company's financial statements as to capital expenditure and revenue expenditure and completeness of recording of any outstanding liabilities relating to the construction.

(vii) expenditure during the year on new restaurant and swimming pool facilities. Whilst the majority of this expenditure would be of a capital nature, it is likely that some would be categorised as revenue (repairs and maintenance) expenditure. There is an inherent risk that material amounts of expenditure may have been incorrectly categorised in the company's financial statements.

(viii) the existence of ongoing repairs, maintenance and replacement programmes for furnishings and equipment. As with (vii) above, inherent risk considerations will focus on the possibility that capital and revenue expenditures have been categorised incorrectly in the company's financial statements.

(ix) the existence of small valuable and desirable non-current asset items. The nature of the hotel business is such that plant and equipment items owned by the business are open to loss due to misappropriation or theft by dishonest individuals. This would represent an increased inherent risk in the area of non-current assets of the financial statements.

(x) compensation claim arising from food poisoning at a company hotel. The inherent risk associated with this event is twofold. Firstly there is a risk that the provision included in the financial statements for the payment of compensation will be materially misstated. Secondly there is the risk (possibly remote) that the food poisoning event may have a catastrophic effect on the reputation of the company's hotels generally, resulting in a downturn of activity. As such it is possible that the company was not a 'going concern' at the statement of financial position date and there is a consequent risk that this fact is not reflected in Finch Co's financial statements as at 30 November 20X7.

(c) General controls as applied to a computer-based accounting system are policies and procedures that relate to the application and support the effective functioning of applications controls by helping to ensure the continuous proper operations of information systems. Examples of such controls include those over data centres and network operations, systems software acquisition, change and maintenance, access security; and application systems acquisition, development and maintenance. The objectives of general controls are to ensure the proper development and implementation of applications, and the integrity of program and data files, and of computer operations.

18 WILLIAMS

Risks of misstatement	Action to be taken
Non-current asset additions	
• Two non-current assets have been recorded as one figure. The assets may have very different useful lives.	• Investigate whether the costs have been individually identified for the purpose of the depreciation calculations.
• The moulding machine may have a short life.	• Investigate the useful life of the moulding machine. Consider whether it can be adapted in the future to deal with changes in technology.
	• Take notice of repairs, costs and regularity of breakdown.
• Currency exchange loss or gain could be incorrectly accounted for on assets with deferred payment dates.	• Agree terms of payment to original contract.
• The assets should be capitalised according to the rate of exchange ruling at 1 March 20X2 and any gain or loss written off against profits.	• Obtain a list of exchange rates and verify calculation of currency loss or gain across the 60-day payment period.
• Too much employee wage costs could be incorrectly capitalised in the cost of the conveyor asset.	• Obtain schedule of conveyor costs. Check that only relevant items are included.
	• Support wage costs by timesheet details.
• The allocation of overheads to the self-constructed asset needs confirmation.	• Check for absorption of overheads at a realistic rate.
	• Compare conveyor costs to market price of similar product.
	• Scrutinise gross profit for unexplained increase.
	• Obtain directors representations in respect of the allocation of costs.

Risks of misstatement	Action to be taken
• The conveyor may have a short useful life if the quality is not good. There is a risk of under depreciating the asset.	• Establish what experience the employees have in building such an asset. • Look at evidence of continuous breakdowns. • Physically inspect the asset to ensure in working order.
• Risk that components acquired have also been included as inventory.	• Obtain list of components required for the conveyor. Agree to the schedule of non-current asset additions. • Ensure no evidence of such items in the closing inventory list.
• The grant could be incorrectly accounted for i.e. non-compliance with standard accounting practice.	• As the grant has been approved but not paid yet a receivables and deferred income account could be created in the statement of financial position. • Check that the cash was received after date. • Establish whether an amount of deferred income has been written off to profits in accordance with the useful life of the assets, matching the depreciation charge. • Determine whether there are any claw back provisions attached to the grant. • Obtain a copy of the approval notice together with grant application report and review for agreement of amounts due. • Check that the accounting policy adopted has been correctly disclosed in the financial statements.

19 JIP

Six matters that should be discussed at the audit meeting are the following:

- The proposed timetable for the final audit, including the date of the inventory count (and who will attend it) and the planned date when the audit is intended to be finished so that the audited financial statements can be published.
- The overall results from the interim audit. Were the tested controls found to be satisfactory in all respects? It may be that some areas were found to be satisfactory and can be reduced in testing at the final audit, while other areas must be substantively tested in full.
- The branches to be visited. It is normal for a business to be operated as a head office with several outlying branches. The audit manager can explain his plan of which branches to visit this year, perhaps using a rotational basis involving visiting all the branches over a number of years.

ANSWERS TO PRACTICE QUESTIONS : SECTION 4

- Changes since the interim audit. Where there have been systems changes, the new system should be discussed and the audit approach decided towards testing the old and the new systems.

- Materiality levels. The audit manager should give an indication of the sizes of errors that he regards as material. Errors above this level would be discussed with management, urging that the figure should be restated. Errors below this level would be noted in the audit working papers in a schedule of unadjusted errors, in case a number of individually immaterial errors accumulate together to become a material amount needing adjustment.

- Any special circumstances applying to working methods when carrying out the audit work at the premises of JIP.

20 ARNOLD

Client:	Arnold	W/P Ref:	A1/1
Y/E Date:	30 June 20X8	Prepared by:	RRT
		Date:	3 January 20X8
		Reviewed by	GL
		Date:	6 January 20X8

Subject: Planning – Inherent Risk Considerations

There are a number of factors relating to Arnold which affect the level of inherent risk. These are as follows:

(i) Cosmetic industry

The industry is subject to fluctuating customer demand. This has a corresponding effect on net realisable value of inventory. Government regulations relating to product Safety Standards could lead to going concern considerations.

(ii) Products not sold under the name of Arnold

Demand for the company's product is dependent upon the success of the customer's own marketing. Here also, this impacts upon inventory valuations.

(iii) Management change

The business is a long established family business. With the retirement of the family member and new external appointments the company must be happy that this will not affect future trading relationships.

(iv) Part-time accountant

The age of the finance director and the request for a part time job suggests that the job had become too onerous. This could mean an increased risk of errors creeping into the financial statements until the full time replacement arrives next year.

(v) Proposed flotation

Declining profitability at a time when growth is needed, if a flotation is to be successful, must mean that there is increased risk of intentional misstatements in the accounts.

KAPLAN PUBLISHING

(vi) Incentive schemes

The productivity bonus may lead to over production of cosmetic inventory, the resale value of which depends upon elastic customer demand. The valuation of inventory and bonus accruals will need careful review. The incentive scheme is only available to certain people and therefore bonus eligibility will need to be considered.

Overall, I would consider this to be a high risk engagement.

21 WIZZIN

The declining profits could create going concern problems that might affect the truth and fairness of the financial statements. There could also be indirect problems if the directors feel that they have to overstate profit in order to conceal the company's trading difficulties.

The company has large amounts of cash flowing through its shops, most of which are dispersed throughout the country and which are staffed in part by part-time employees whose backgrounds would be difficult to check. Staff fraud could be a problem.

The nature of the business could be affected by economic swings. Builders might not need materials if there is a downturn. Consumers might not be willing to spend on home improvements. That could create further pressures for the directors to overstate revenues and profits.

Each shop has large quantities of valuable and moveable plant that could be a target for staff fraud. These items might also be difficult to depreciate accurately because their useful lives will be affected by the care with which they are used and maintained by staff at branch level.

The company has borrowed heavily and the directors might be tempted to smooth profits and cash flows in order to satisfy bank covenants. This could also create going concern problems because the company might not be able to borrow further if it runs into temporary difficulties.

22 YES HOUSES

Good audit planning is essential to the satisfactory and effective performance of an audit and the auditor should consider the timetable and staff allocation at this stage.

The auditor needs to be able to ensure that he allocates the correct staff to the appropriate work; there would be little use in allocating a new junior member of staff to the audit of contingencies which can be a very judgmental area, or an area of complexity such as computer auditing. At the planning stages of the audit the auditor needs to be able to identify actual or potential problems and consider actions to be taken.

The auditor also needs to establish an overall audit plan which is then monitored to ensure that each task and thus the audit is efficiently and effectively completed. The establishment of an overall plan can clearly therefore assist with controlling the audit. By adequately planning the auditor should be able to identify at which stages he may need to use specialist staff or independent third parties and can therefore ensure that they are consulted as and when necessary. By identifying the type and extent of work to be performed he can also ensure that any preliminary work that needs to be performed in advance is completed when necessary.

ANSWERS TO PRACTICE QUESTIONS : SECTION 4

23 MATERIALITY

(a) ISA 320 *Materiality in Planning and Performing an Audit* explains the characteristics of materiality:

'Misstatements, including omissions are considered to be material if they individually or in the aggregate, could reasonably be expected to influence the economic decisions of users taken on the basis of the financial statements;

Judgements about materiality are made in light of surrounding circumstances, and are affected by the size or nature of a misstatement, or a combination of both; and

Judgements about matters that are material to users of financial statements are based on a consideration of the common financial information needs of users as a group. The possible effect of misstatements on specific individual users, whose needs may vary widely is not considered'.

Materiality is not capable of general mathematical definition as it has both qualitative and quantitative aspects.

(b) Materiality is an important concept for auditors, as it acknowledges the fact that accounts cannot be perfectly accurate, and so allows small errors. If accounts had to be perfectly accurate, auditors would have to check every transaction.

Materiality allows an auditor to base audit tests on samples of items, the results of which are analysed to estimate the maximum level of error in the population as a whole. Provided this error is not material the auditor can accept the figure.

Materiality also allows an auditor to accept figures that are based on management estimates and assumptions provided the errors are unlikely to exceed materiality thresholds. In this way the number of items checked in an audit is a small percentage of the total transactions, and the audit is completed at a reasonable cost.

24 TIGHTROPE

(a) Reasons for increase in time spent on audit work

(i) New non-current assets

- Initial discussion with the directors over treatment of these assets. This would have taken expensive partner and manager time.

- Decision on valuation. Some assets are difficult to value, and yet they must be reviewed regularly in case their value has been impaired. An acceptable valuation method, in accordance with generally agreed accounting practices, which the auditor would have to review, would have to be agreed with the client.

- Disclosure in the financial statements would need to be in accordance with relevant company law and any generally agreed accounting practice. The auditor would need to ensure that the financial statements agreed with these.

- Depreciation. Agreement would be needed on the depreciation rate, which again may be difficult.

(ii) Upgrade of computer system

The extent of the upgrade is not identified here i.e. was a new system purchased, or only some new software for an existing system. Depending on the extent of the upgrade the following will become more significant:

- verification of new system, including recording the system, identifying controls and testing these with tests of control;
- agreement of balances transferred between the systems, including direct one-for-one checks as well as global control total checking;
- ensuring new system operated correctly by a parallel run. Results of both systems would be compared and differences investigated;
- audit of two systems. It is likely that more testing would be done than would be necessary with only one system;
- update of permanent file with new systems information;
- use of computer audit department if the new system was complicated enough to warrant this.

All these factors will result in increased time on the audit this year and therefore increased cost to the client.

(iii) Suppliers' statements not agreeing

Audit costs have been increased due to the increased amount of time spent on a detailed payables circularisation. This is necessary because:

- the auditor needs confirmation that each area of the statement of financial position is materially correct;
- the failure to reconcile some supplier statements indicates to the auditor that there may be a material error;
- more testing has to be performed to ensure that there is not a material error.

(iv) Misappropriation of payroll funds

During audit planning, the auditor attempts to identify areas in the financial statements where material error could occur. The payroll is a higher risk area this year due to the fraud that has been carried out. Additional audit testing is therefore required to ensure that:

- the fraud has been completely identified;
- the wages system has been improved to prevent future fraud occurring.

Both of these activities will mean increased audit time, the first due to increased testing, and the latter due to additional review of the system and discussion concerning the controls with management.

(b) Auditors must always perform audits in accordance with auditing standards. If these standards are not maintained then the auditor would become liable to legal action either from his client, the company, or from shareholders, for negligent auditing. Fee pressure should therefore not be a factor in deciding the amount of time required to perform an audit adequately. If fee pressure is such that the minimum time required is not available to the auditor, then the client should be informed of this, and, if necessary, the auditor will have to decline to act for that client, rather than compromise his standards.

Time efficiencies may be generated by identifying risk areas during the planning phase of the audit, or by the use of technology which decreases time during audit work, like, for example, the production of audit programmes and other documentation. These time savings may then be passed onto the client.

It is above all necessary for the auditor to keep the client fully aware of the reasons for his costs and so minimise pressure from the client in this area.

25 AUDIT RISK

I would consider the following matters when I consider the audit risk relating to the items in the question:

(i) For tangible non-current assets, the audit risk will be higher when they have a large value, or when the non-current assets may be worth materially less than the value shown in the statement of financial position. Although the value of land and buildings is likely to be quite large, their market value should be higher than the value in the accounts, particularly if they have been acquired many years ago and have not been revalued recently. Non-current assets may be worth substantially less than their carrying value when they are obsolete or have to be sold at a loss. This will include companies which are making losses, those which are having going concern problems and those where a certain activity, which uses the non-current asset, is being discontinued or is likely to be discontinued.

Machinery has a higher risk of obsolescence where:

- it is used to produce a specialised product which may go out of fashion, or be replaced by another product which requires different equipment;
- it is high technology equipment which is more likely to become obsolete.

Also, the company may fail to get it operating satisfactorily, the supplier may go out of business, or it may be impossible to repair because either the replacement parts are no longer available or no further service support is provided (this sometimes happens with computers).

There may be a high risk where finance leased equipment is included in the statement of financial position and the company is having going concern problems. On liquidation the equipment will not belong to the company.

(ii) Inventory has a high level of audit risk in most companies as it usually has a material value in the financial statements. Inventory is a high risk area as its value is entered in the accounts at the year end, and it is not maintained as an accounting record like trade receivables. Frequently inventory quantities are found only at the physical inventory count, and the value per unit may be worth less than cost, yet it may have been valued at cost. In manufacturing companies inventory value will be more difficult to determine than in other companies, as it includes direct labour cost and production overheads. Old inventory will probably have to be valued at net realisable value, and some of this inventory may be worth only scrap value. This inventory will include raw materials, work in progress and finished goods for products the company no longer sells. Some of this inventory may arise because more inventory was purchased than was used in production. The valuation of specialised inventories, and spare parts (e.g. for cars) may be difficult, particularly if they have been in inventory a long time.

(iii) In most manufacturing companies, receivables have a lower risk than inventory and payables. The audit risk is mainly related to the level of irrecoverable debts the company incurs. There will be a lower risk where a company sells to large companies, rather than to a large number of small businesses. There is a greater risk when debts are old, when the company has many new customers or when the general age of the company's receivables is increasing. If the company sells goods subject to reservation of title, this will reduce the risk of irrecoverable debts, provided the retention of title clause is legally enforceable.

(iv) Payables are likely to be a higher risk than receivables. The main risk is that certain payables may have been omitted. Usually, this arises from poor records of receipt of goods, inadequate matching of invoices to goods received, or poor systems for following up differences between suppliers' statements and the purchase ledger balances. The risk will be relatively high where the company has a large number of outstanding disputes with suppliers (e.g. for short delivery of goods, quality problems and pricing disputes). Trade payables are frequently a problem where a company is having going concern problems, as there may be inadequate recording of transactions and round-sum payments to payables make reconciling suppliers' statements more difficult.

(v) Contingencies will have high risk where large claims for damages are being made against the client. Also, contingencies can be important where an activity of the business is being terminated. In this situation there may be claims by employees, customers, suppliers and amounts due on termination of leases. Claims for damages can arise for many reasons. These include damage to another person's property (e.g. in extracting minerals), claims by employees resulting from damage to their health, claims by competitors for alleged infringement of their copyrights, and fines due to contravention of the law. Also, in some types of business, such as civil engineering construction, there is a potential liability for claims arising from using faulty materials (e.g. the use of high asbestos cement in the construction of buildings). Claims arising from faulty products can be very substantial, particularly if the fault has resulted in loss of life, such as claims arising from aircraft accidents. Contingencies can be a high risk area, as it is easy to fail to detect the risk of a potential liability, and even if the potential claim is highlighted, it can be very difficult to quantify the sum it will cost the company.

26 BRAHMS CO

Key answer tips

Ensure that you answer both elements of the question requirement – dealing with a risk-based approach and also dealing with the audit risk model.

Audit risk is the risk that the auditor expresses an inappropriate audit opinion when the financial statements are materially misstated. An auditor adopting a risk-based auditing **approach obtains an understanding of an entity and its environment, and having assessed** the risks of material misstatements in the financial statements at the assertion level, directs audit resources to the risky areas as appropriate.

Auditors use the audit risk model to identify the elements of audit risk and to start to plan the audit strategy to minimise those risks. The three elements of audit risk are:

Inherent risk

This is the susceptibility of an assertion to a misstatement that could be material, either individually or when aggregated with other misstatements, assuming that there were no related controls.

Control risk

This is the risk that a misstatement that could occur in an assertion and that could be material, either individually or when aggregated with other misstatements, will not be prevented, or detected and corrected, on a timely basis by the entity's internal control.

Detection risk

Detection risk relates to the nature, timing and extent of the auditor's procedures. It is the risk that the auditor will not detect a misstatement that exists in an assertion that could be material individually or when aggregated with other misstatements. It is the function of the effectiveness of an audit procedure and of its application by the auditor.

In practice, the auditor sets the level of audit risk required. Inherent risk and control risk factors are set for each individual client, leaving detection risk as the balancing figure. A high detection risk indicates limited audit testing (the auditor places high reliance on the control systems) while low detection risk indicates significant audit testing as the risk of error is higher (poor control systems).

27 MOZART CO

The purpose of audit working papers is to record information relating to a specific audit, on the planning of the audit work, the nature, timing and extent of audit procedures performed, the results thereof, and the conclusions drawn from the audit evidence obtained. Audit working papers record an auditor's reasoning in arriving at conclusions on specific areas of an entity's financial statements. This, together with other information included in the working papers, could be useful in the event of there being litigation against the audit firm in connection with the audit or for the planning of future audits.

The extent of working papers to be prepared is a matter for the professional judgement of the auditor, and will depend on the auditor's assessment of risk attaching to the audit assignment and the extent of substantive procedures carried out. It is generally accepted that the working papers prepared and retained should be sufficient such that they would provide another auditor, who has no previous connection with the audit, with an understanding of the work performed and the basis of the principal decisions taken.

28 TULIP CO

(a) When evaluating the control environment of an entity, an auditor should consider the following matters:

(i) Communication and enforcement of integrity and ethical values – essential elements which influence the effectiveness of the design, administration and monitoring of controls.

(ii) Commitment to competence – management's consideration of the competence levels for particular jobs and how those levels translate into requisite skills and knowledge.

(iii) Management's philosophy and operating style – management's approach to taking and managing business risks, and management's attitudes and actions towards financial reporting, information processing and accounting functions and personnel.

(iv) Organisational structure – the framework within which an entity's activities for achieving its objectives are planned, executed, controlled and reviewed.

(v) Assignment of authority and responsibility – how authority and responsibility for operating activities are assigned and how reporting relationships and authorisation hierarchies are established.

(vi) Human resources policies and practices – recruitment, orientation, training, evaluating, counselling, promoting, compensating and remedial actions.

(**Note:** Full marks will be awarded for identifying FOUR of the above or other appropriate matters.)

(b) (i) The areas on which my firm should obtain detailed information include:

- The various income streams of Tulip Co. These may include for example, income from the provision of accommodation and from the sale of meals, refreshments and souvenirs.
- Information about the market in which Tulip Co operates, for example, the size of the market, major competitors, the company's market share, pricing policies and the marketing strategy and objectives of the company.
- Information about the way the company conducts its operations, for example, the range of adventure holidays offered, advance booking incentives for customers and details of expanding and declining activities.
- The extent of the company's involvement in electronic commerce, including internet sales and marketing activities.
- The geographic spread of the activities of the company and the type and extent of activity at each location.
- Employment practices within the adventure holiday sector generally and within the company, for example, the employment of specialist staff, use of temporary 'seasonal staff', staff training issues and remuneration levels within the sector.
- Details of the company's cost structures, including accommodation costs, employment costs, indemnity insurance costs and those relating to general administration.
- Details of any alliances or joint venture activities entered into by the company together with details of any activities outsourced to third parties.

(**Note:** Full marks will be awarded to answers identifying any SIX of the above or other relevant matters.)

(ii) The benefits of using document flowcharts to record a company's accounting and internal control systems are that they:

- enable the systems to be recorded in a standard format which is easily understood by specialist and non-specialist audit staff;
- present systems information in a logical sequence;

- highlight relationships between different parts of a system;
- provide an overview of a system such that superfluous documents, bottlenecks and weaknesses are more easily identified;
- encourage a disciplined approach to the recording of a system in that the originator of a flowchart must have a good understanding of the system being recorded.

(**Note:** Full marks will be awarded for stating THREE of the above or other perceived advantages.)

29 PARKER

Over-trading

The turnover of Parker is growing quite rapidly, although this growth is not matched in net profits. The company has been expanding into the Internet, and plans to introduce other product lines for sale in this division. There is the risk that the business will exhaust any cash reserves as it continues to expand but does not generate sufficient additional cash to pay for that expansion. In this situation suppliers may go unpaid and at the extreme the business will be forced into liquidation. Therefore the financial statements may not adequately disclose doubts about going concern.

Internet trading

The decision to expand the Internet business may cause other problems for Parker. Selling of books and CDs appear to be related as they are both forms of entertainment and the customer knows what the product is like. Selling toys may fall into a similar category, but garden furniture and clothes are different. Garden furniture is bulky and will certainly cost more to deliver while clothes are sold more on taste and a high level of returns can be expected. Specific risks with this decision therefore relate to the overall ability of management to run the business given their apparent lack of knowledge of Internet trading the need to setup and manage systems for the sales of many new products the need to allow for a much larger volume of returns the possibility of inventory obsolescence if Parker overstocks on clothes which go 'out of fashion'.

Control environment

The whole environment in which the control systems should be operating appears weak. There are errors in the systems, the extent of which are not known, and the directors and the accountant do not appear to be inclined to attempt to remedy the situation. The skills of the accountant may also be questioned because he appears to have been appointed not on merit, but from some personal relationship with the directors. Other errors may also have occurred which have not been detected. The risk is that the financial statements may have material errors in them.

Bank loan

The directors require additional finance to expand the business. To provide this finance it is likely that the bank will require sight of the audited financial statements; the directors of Parker expect the audit to be completed prior to meeting the bank. The auditor may need to write to the bank to disclaim reliance on the audit report for the purposes of making a bank loan. There is a risk to the audit firm of being sued if the bank relies on the report and sustains financial loss. There is also a risk to Parker that the loan is not obtained and the company goes into liquidation. The financial statements may need to be prepared on a breakup basis.

First year of audit

The audit is also risky for the audit firm because it is the first year of an audit and the client has expectations about the type of auditor's report to be produced. The accounting systems also appear to be unreliable, again increasing the risk of material error. The audit firm must ensure that sufficient time and resources are allocated to the audit to ensure that the audit opinion can be supported. Pressure from the directors to complete the audit quickly will have to be resisted.

ACCOUNTING SYSTEMS AND CONTROLS (INCLUDING COMPUTER-BASED SYSTEMS)

GENERAL PRINCIPLES

30 DS

(a) The internal control system is the collection of procedures put in place by management which is intended to ensure that the business is run in an orderly and efficient manner. Such a system would give management some confidence that their policies were being complied with, that the business' assets were reasonably safe, that the accounting records were relatively free from irregularities and that, ultimately, they could state that the financial statements give a true and fair view.

(b) Examples of control procedures and example of a specific procedure include:

Control procedures	Example of a specific procedure
Approval and control of documents	The signing of purchase orders by authorised staff in the buying department to show that all purchases have been authorised.
Controls over computerised operations and the IT environment	Everyone logging on to a computer system is required to have a valid password and user ID. All users have restricted access to those areas that they need for their official duties.
Checking the arithmetical accuracy of the records	The accounts packages might have a number of checks built in. For example, the parts of an invoice must sum to the total amount input, otherwise the transaction will not be processed by the system.
Comparing the results of cash, security and inventory counts with accounting records	Conducting spot checks of inventory at a given location for comparison with the inventory records to get a proper idea of losses through shoplifting, staff fraud, etc.
Comparing internal data with external sources of information	Agreeing the details from suppliers' statements to their accounts on the purchase ledger and ensuring that all differences are legitimate timing differences.
Limiting direct physical access to assets and records	All tills should be locked when not in use. Staff should sign for till keys and be responsible for all cash taken.

31 WOODS

Non-current assets accounting system

Tutorial note

Although only THREE control objectives were requested in the question, five have been provided to aid learning.

Control objective	Control
To ensure that all non-current asset disposals are properly authorised	Proper documentation should be completed and authorised by nominated authorised individuals prior to any disposal.
To ensure that all non-current asset purchases are properly authorised	Purchase Orders for non-current assets should be signed by nominated authorised individuals; copies of sample signatures should be held by the finance department for verification against the purchase order
To ensure that all non-current assets are maintained in a secure environment to prevent any misuse/misappropriation	Spot checks of non-current assets should be regularly performed by nominated individuals and reconciled to the non-current asset register.
To ensure that depreciation rates are appropriate	The depreciation rates used should be authorised by a nominated senior individual and should be consistent with GAAP.
To ensure that where non-current assets are income yielding that the income is properly recorded.	An independent reconciliation should be performed to verify that all income receivable has been correctly posted.

32 FOREST

Sales and receivables accounting system

Tutorial note

Although only THREE control objectives were requested in the question, seven have been provided to aid learning.

Control objective	Control
To ensure that all sales (on credit) are made to creditworthy customers; and all sales are to bona fide customers	Prior to sales of any goods on credit, checks should be performed to verify their creditworthiness, for example by interrogating on-line company history systems or obtaining bank references, obtaining copy of previous year's financial statements.

Control objective	Control
To ensure that all sales are properly accounted for in the company's accounting records	All invoices should be sequential and pre-numbered; sequence checks should be performed during processing to identify any discrepancies.
To ensure that all credit notes are authorised	Credit notes should be authorised by nominated senior individuals; supporting documentation should be completed to support the validity of the reason for the credit notes.
To ensure that all debts are collected as they fall due	Receivable accounts should be regularly reviewed to ensure payment is received on time or followed up on a timely basis when not.
To ensure that all irrecoverable debts written off are authorised prior to write off	Only nominated, authorised individuals should be able to perform debt write offs and only after there is no possibility of debt recovery.
To ensure that goods delivered are consistent with those ordered by the customer	Prior to delivery to the customer the goods should be checked to the sales order form, and a despatch note completed.
To ensure that customers are invoiced on a timely basis for goods sold at the correct price	Targets should be set for invoice processing (from despatch date) such as 'maximum 4 days', and these targets monitored to ensure compliance. An independent check should be performed on invoices to confirm that the prices are accurate and any special terms agreed have been correctly incorporated.

33 SHOW

(a) The primary duty of the external auditor is to examine the financial statements of an enterprise and to issue a report on the 'truth and fairness' of those financial statements. It is not the external auditors' responsibility to detect all fraud.

However, whilst there is no specified duty to search for fraud, it is required by the auditing profession that the auditors plan and carry out their audit work in a manner which enables them to have a reasonable expectation of detecting material misstatement in the financial statements arising from fraud and error.

External auditors will typically face inherent difficulties in the detection of fraud. Some of the reasons for this are:

- Fraud (by its very nature) is usually accompanied by acts specifically designed to conceal its existence.
- It often involves collusion between employees. If senior employees are involved, internal controls which may generally be considered to be effective may be avoided.

- Additionally, employees may try to 'play the system'. If they are aware that auditors are primarily interested in detecting material misstatements, employees carrying out fraudulent acts may ensure that any losses fall beneath the materiality level used by the auditors. These losses are unlikely to be revealed during normal audit testing.

We can apply the principles outlined above to Show as follows:

- Three senior managers were involved in the making of the fraudulent payment to the supplier. It is possible that these managers worked in collusion to bypass the company's internal controls when making the payments. It is also likely that they worked together to deceive the external auditors.
- All of the fraudulent payments were relatively small in amount. This may have been 'planned' by the managers so that they would not draw the attention of the external auditors to the payments. In the absence of any specific cause for concern the external auditors would not be put 'on enquiry' in respect of the payments.
- In these circumstances it is perhaps understandable that the external auditors did not detect the fraud.

(b) **Note:** FOUR points only are required by the question.

The limitations of any internal control system include:

- The cost of implementing a specific control may be disproportionate to the potential loss which may result from its absence – in which case the control is unlikely to be implemented.
- Most internal controls procedures are directed at everyday transactions rather than non-routine transactions.
- The existence of human error due to carelessness, distraction, mistakes of judgement and the misunderstanding of instructions.
- The possibility of the avoidance of controls through collusion with other parties.
- The possibility that a person responsible for operating all control could abuse the system, for example by overriding or bypassing controls.
- The possibility that procedures may become inadequate or out of date due to changes in circumstances.
- Management and staff may become 'complacent' over time, with the result that the level of compliance with control procedures deteriorates.

34 DOORS

(a) The objectives which internal controls relating to an accounting system should achieve include ensuring that:

- all transactions are carried out in accordance with proper levels of authority set by the directors of the company;
- all transactions and other events are completely and accurately recorded on a timely basis.

>
>
> *Tutorial note*
>
> *The requirement for this part of the question asked for two objectives. Answers other than those listed above would be acceptable, including the following.*

- The company's assets are safeguarded against loss, damage or fraudulent activity.
- Recorded assets are compared with existing assets on a regular basis and appropriate action is taken with regard to any differences.
- Information extracted from the accounting records permits the company's financial statements to be prepared in accordance with the applicable reporting framework.

(b) (i) The directors of Doors would require that recorded trade receivables balances were all collectable, that they are collected in good time and that irrecoverable debts were being avoided as far as possible. Procedures should therefore be in place to meet these requirements.

In order to achieve these objectives credit transactions should be subject to appropriate settlement terms, which are both appropriate to Doors but are not too unattractive to the company's customers. In addition, in order to maintain the company's cash flow position and minimise the possibility of irrecoverable debts, any significant delay in payments being received from receivables should be subject to the company's established follow up procedures including possible litigation to recover payment.

Similarly, balances outstanding from customers who have exceeded their normal credit terms should be investigated and followed up by the company's credit control staff, independent of sales and sales accounting staff. The independent status of credit control staff should assist in ensuring that outstanding balances have not arisen as a consequence of fraudulent acts.

Sales ledger balances should be extracted from the sales ledger and aged analysis prepared on a regular basis. This will enable 'problem' accounts to be identified and a decision can then be made as to whether a doubtful debts provision should be made against outstanding receivable balances.

(ii) The directors of Doors require assurance that the company's plant and equipment is safeguarded from loss, damage or the effects of fraudulent activity. In addition, they require assurance that there is completeness of accounting records and that the assets are recorded at their proper value.

As certain items of the company's plant and equipment are both portable and potentially 'attractive' there is a relatively high risk of loss due to unauthorised removal by employees or a third party.

Similarly, whilst the company's depreciation policy will have the objective of depreciating plant and equipment over the useful economic lives of the assets, this may not be achieved in practice. Intensive use, damage or breakdown, may result in asset values being materially overstated in the financial statements. It is therefore of fundamental importance that the company's plant and equipment assets are regularly inspected and that any necessary adjustments to the accounting records are made.

Designated responsible employees of the company, who should not have any responsibility for the purchase, custody or disposal of non-current assets, should carry out inspections.

All items should be inspected regularly – this could be carried out on a rotational basis – and any discrepancies with regard to the physical existence or condition of assets should be reported to senior management for investigation and follow up.

(iii) Two main aspects arise here. Firstly, it is important that, if an individual is absent from the workplace, the flow of work in their area should not be interrupted as this may result in delays in the processing of significant accounting transactions.

Secondly, the availability of another employee to take on the work of the absent member of staff will result in the work of one employee being checked by another, with the possibility that any irregularities, which may have arisen, will come to light. Knowledge that such a procedure is in operation in the organisation may act as a deterrent, discouraging employees from non-compliance with company procedures.

35 ROSE CO

(a) As with any operating company, in order for Rose Co to function successfully the directors of the company must ensure that the company's operations are effective and efficient, that it complies with applicable laws and regulations and that it has a reliable financial reporting system. If the company does not have an effective system of internal control, then it is probable that corporate objectives, with regard to these matters, will not be met, thus adversely affecting the successful functioning of the company.

(**Note:** Full marks will be awarded to answers containing the above or other appropriate points.)

(b) Internal controls, no matter how well designed and operated, can provide an entity with only reasonable assurance about achieving the entity's financial reporting objectives. The likelihood of achievement is affected by limitations inherent to internal control. These include the realities that human judgement in decision-making can be faulty and that breakdowns in internal control can occur because of human failures, such as simple errors or mistakes. Errors also may occur in the use of information produced by I.T. For example, automated controls may be designed to report transactions over a specified amount for management review, but individuals responsible for conducting the review may not understand the purpose of such reports and, accordingly, may fail to review them or investigate unusual items.

Additionally, controls can be circumvented by the collusion of two or more people or inappropriate management override of internal control. For example, management may enter into side agreements with customers that alter the terms and conditions of the entity's standard sales contracts, which may result in improper revenue recognition. Also, exception checks in a software program that are designed to identify and report transactions that exceed specified credit limits may be overridden or disabled.

Further inherent limitations in any system of internal control include the possibility that procedures may become inadequate due to changes in conditions – for example, in a company experiencing rapid growth in sales, existing control activities may be inadequate to cope with the volume of sales transactions. Additionally, there is an inherent weakness in any internal control system that is directed at routine transactions rather than non-routine transactions. For example, an accounting system which does not incorporate sufficient controls to properly identify and process transactions relating to the purchase of non-current assets, is inherently weak.

(**Note:** Full marks will be awarded to answers not necessarily containing all of the above points.)

(c)

Tutorial note

In answering this type of question, try to think of arguments both for and against the statement, i.e. the auditors would be negligent if they discovered suspicious circumstances but did nothing about them etc., and they would not be negligent if the fraud were immaterial, etc.

The amount of money defrauded from the company of $9,682 during the year ended 31 January 20X6 represents less than 1% of reported net profit and is therefore not material in the context of the disclosures made in the financial statements of Rose Co. However the fact that the fraud was committed is indicative of a problem with the day-to-day systems of control within the company and the directors are therefore justified in having concerns about this.

From the auditors' perspective, unless their audit of Rose Co's financial statements revealed evidence to the contrary, they were entitled to assume that there was no fraudulent activity during the year. However, they should have planned and performed their audit procedures with an attitude of professional scepticism recognising that conditions or events could be found indicating fraudulent activity.

It is generally recognised that it is often difficult to detect fraudulent activity when it is perpetrated by two senior managers of a company who collude to conceal the losses consequently incurred. Given that the total sum defrauded from Rose Co amounts to $9,682 over a six-month (mid-year) period, it is probable that the fraud was carefully orchestrated by the financial director and the senior manager, so that only small individual amounts were targeted for fraud at a time when it was unlikely that the auditors would be present at the company. Given these factors and the immateriality of the sum involved, then providing a review of the auditors' working papers does not reveal inadequacies in their audit procedures, it is unlikely that the auditors would be found to have been negligent in not detecting the fraud. Consequently the directors' assertion appears to be unjustified.

(**Note:** Full marks will be awarded to answers not necessarily containing all of the above points.)

ASCERTAINING AND RECORDING THE SYSTEM

36 HOCATTA

Tutorial note

Although only FOUR methods of ascertaining the accounting system were requested in the question, five have been provided to aid learning.

The methods I may use to ascertain the accounting system for the purchase of motorcycles include:

- I will ask the purchasing manager and other staff involved in the purchasing system to describe the system to me. By asking different members of staff this should highlight any discrepancies in their understanding as to how the system operates.

- I will inspect any systems manual that Hocatta may have. The manual should describe the system in detail and enable me to gain a clear understanding as to how the purchasing system operates. I will ensure that the manual is the latest up-to-date version before placing any reliance on it.

- I will observe members of staff involved in the system carrying out their daily purchases routines. This will enable me to compare employees in actual operation with what I have been told happens. I would need to be aware that Hocatta employees may have been warned by management that I may be observing them and that they should ensure they follow documented procedures.

- I will inspect last year's purchasing system notes and compare them with the system I have documented to identify any changes to the system recorded last year. Last year's system notes will be retained in the permanent audit file.

- Once I have identified the purchasing system I will carry out a walkthrough test i.e. select a small sample of transactions and trace them through the purchasing system from the beginning to the end of the system that I have identified.

FAU: FOUNDATIONS IN AUDIT

REVENUE AND RECEIVABLES

37 CAR PARKING

(a)

Client:	Car Park Co.	W/P Ref:	E1/1
Y/E Date:	31 December 20X8	Prepared by:	RRT
		Date:	3 May 20X8
		Reviewed by:	GL
		Date:	6 May X8

Audit programme: Tests of control (income)

Objective: To ensure adequacy of controls of system of accounting for completeness of income

	W/P Ref	Performed by	Reviewed by
(i) For a sample of days, check that parking tickets have been signed as evidence of the fee charged having been checked by head office personnel. The cash banked per the statement should be agreed to the summary of fees taken.			
(ii) For a sample of parking tickets, check that the issue from, and subsequent return to, head office was controlled, and that any missing tickets were fully investigated.			

(b) Test (i) would indicate whether all income due had been properly recorded and received.

Test (ii) would indicate whether all tickets resulted in income being received and recorded.

38 GREEN

Substantive procedures that should be carried out to verify irrecoverable debts include:

(i) Ask the sales manager for a schedule of irrecoverable debts that make up the total in the accounts. Add up the figures and agree the balance to the irrecoverable debts total in the financial statements.

(ii) Inspect all customer files and correspondence relating to each customer deemed an irrecoverable debt to ensure that sufficient effort has been made by Green to recover the debt. This may include inspecting solicitor's letters and debt collection agency correspondence.

(iii) Inspect the aged debt's analysis to identify any debts still outstanding e.g. more than 60 days old. Ask the sales manager why the old debts are still outstanding and what action is Green taking to recover the debts. Consider if the doubtful debt provision is sufficient in light of the old debts identified.

(iv) Ask the sales manager how he has calculated the doubtful debt provision in the financial statements e.g. specific overdue or disputed invoices identified. Recalculate the provision and confirm the figure in the financial statements is correct.

(v) Review the results of the circularisation of receivables to determine whether they indicate that a write-off or allowance may be required.

(vi) Review cash received after the accounting year end to determine whether any debts that may be considered bad have actually been recovered.

39 LONDGLAS & CO

Four factors influencing inherent risk include:

(i) *The directors of the company own all of the share capital of Wilsun*

As all of the directors own the company the auditors will be reporting to the directors in their capacity as shareholders. This means that there are no external shareholders for the directors to be concerned about. This could lead to the directors manipulating the financial statements for their own benefit e.g. changing accounting policies to increase or decrease overall profit and therefore maximise dividend payments and minimise taxation.

Without external shareholders the directors manage the company's affairs to suit themselves, for example rewarding themselves high salaries and bonuses as directors voted for by themselves as shareholders. This could lead to sales and receivables being potentially overstated and liabilities understated.

As shareholders the directors will ensure that they pay themselves a dividend, even if cash flow is weak. This could lead to payables not being paid as cash is directed into other areas. The long term implication of this could be to starve the company of cash as the directors extract funds for their own benefit without shareholder resistance.

(ii) *The nature of Wilsun's business*

Wilsun operates in a very volatile market i.e. televisions and DVDs. These items are not purchased as an everyday occurrence and therefore sales may be very irregular i.e. customers buying at certain times of the year such as public holidays.

In addition, competition would be very fierce with many larger high street and internet retailers selling these types of products. This would have an impact on pricing and discounting which the larger retailers could probably absorb better than the smaller retail stores like Wilsun.

If a serious 'price war' developed in the television and DVD market between retailers then Wilsun may not be able to survive the impact with only four stores and its future survival could be in question.

Televisions and DVDs are fairly technical items, however, fashion changes all the time e.g. televisions with internet access, which means that Wilsun could be left behind its competitors if the technology changes and Wilsun is unable to change direction quickly and be able to sell the latest high-tech, fashionable televisions and DVD players.

(iii) *Staffing levels/inventory implications*

Wilsun employs large teams of engineers at its stores to repair high quantities of equipment. The cost of employing these skilled engineers might exceed the overall income generated from repair work. This would have a serious impact on cash flow i.e. monthly salaries to be paid, however, customers are not paying for the repairs until collection and the customers may not collect their items for some time after they are repaired.

The high volume of repairs is also a point of concern. Why are so many televisions and DVD players going wrong? Is it that the initial manufacture of these items is poor quality and therefore customers may go elsewhere if their televisions and DVDs keep breaking down when purchased from Wilsun. This inventory issue must be considered by Mr Cool as it could have an impact on inventory valuation.

In addition, the company also employs engineers based at each store to install television aerials supplied by Wilsun. These engineers are again a fixed cost to Wilsun as the salaries are paid regardless of the aerials installed. As television sets are becoming more technical e.g. satellite transmissions, Mr Cool should consider the impact on inventory valuation of obsolete aerials plus the potential redundancy costs if Wilsun needs to make repair and aerial engineers redundant.

(iv) *Potential sale of shares depending on trading results for the current year*

As Wilsun is a private company and the directors are also the shareholders, they will be probably quite keen to sell the company's shares for the best price they can get. Therefore if the final offer price is based upon the company's trading results for the current financial year, the directors may attempt to manipulate the financial statements to ensure they are as attractive as possible to influence the offer price.

Mr Cool must be very aware of this when planning the audit of Wilsun. Audit tests must be designed to ensure that revenue and profit is not overstated and that the statement of financial position does reflect true assets and liabilities.

40 HAYDN CO

(i) **Deficiency**

The sales director and the sales clerks have full access to all trade receivables ledger files.

Implication

As sales department staff are responsible for the authorisation and administration of sales transactions and for recording transaction details in the company's accounting records, there is a high risk of fraud and error arising on the sales and trade receivables area.

Recommendations

The responsibilities for the authorisation, administering and recording of sales transactions in the company's accounting records should be allocated to separate individuals. Recording of sales transactions in the company's accounting records should be carried out only by appropriately experienced accounts department staff. Sales staff should have read-only access to trade receivables ledger files.

(ii) Deficiency

The sales director is responsible for granting credit facilities to new customers.

Implication

The sales director has a vested interest in granting new credit facilities in order to achieve sales targets. He is also in a position to enter into fraudulent arrangements with customers. As a consequence, Haydn Co is exposed to the increased possibility of losses arising from irrecoverable debts and fraudulent transactions.

Recommendations

The responsibility to grant new credit facilities to customers should be vested in a responsible official of the company, segregated from the sales department and recording of transactions in the accounting records.

(iii) Deficiency

Credit limits are not applied to customer accounts.

Implication

There is a strong possibility that Haydn Co will incur irrecoverable debts if appropriate credit limits are not applied to customer accounts and strictly adhered to.

Recommendations

A maximum credit limit should be applied to each customer account, based on a customer's financial strength and ability to pay. Customer accounts should be closely monitored by an independent credit controller to ensure that credit limits are not exceeded.

(iv) Deficiency

The sales director is responsible for pursuing late paying customers.

Implication

Haydn Co's exposure to cash flow difficulties and irrecoverable debts could be increased. This is because the director may have a pre-disposition not to place undue pressure on late paying customers for fear of their withdrawing custom with regard to future stationery purchases. Additionally the director may be exposed to beneficial offers from customers, made to him in his personal capacity, to allow advantageous payment terms on specific customer accounts.

Recommendations

The responsibility for credit control should be vested in a responsible official of the company, who is totally segregated from the authorisation, processing and recording of sales transactions.

(v) Deficiency

Telephone orders are accepted for the despatch of the company's products.

Implication

Haydn Co's exposure to losses is increased as a consequence of goods being despatched in response to unauthorised or bogus telephone orders.

Recommendations

Haydn Co should only accept written orders from *bona fide* customers. Procedures for ordering from Haydn Co should be made clear to all customers, through the issue of terms and conditions of trading, and these should be strictly adhered to by Haydn Co. Any doubts as to the authenticity of written orders received from customers should be removed before execution of those orders.

(vi) Deficiency

Sales clerks have full access to product price data contained in the standing data file of the sales invoicing program.

Implication

The sales clerks are responsible for generating sales invoices to customers and therefore have the opportunity to influence, either fraudulently or erroneously, prices charged for the company's products.

Recommendations

Access to the standing data file containing product price data should be restricted to the sales director and other appropriate senior responsible officials of the company. Strict controls should be exercised over the updating of this information and it should be regularly monitored to ensure that prices on file equate to those on Haydn Co's authorised price list.

(vii) Deficiency

Sales invoices are raised and forwarded to customers prior to the receipt of confirmation that goods have been despatched to customers.

Implication

Sales invoices could be forwarded to customers in the absence of goods being despatched to them. In such instances Haydn Co would be erroneously recognising the revenue from the sales transaction in its accounting records whilst also incorrectly recognising a trade receivable.

Dependent on customers' own internal controls, it is likely that relationships may become strained if customers constantly receive invoices in advance of the receipt of goods ordered.

Recommendations

Current procedures with regard to the production of sales invoices and goods despatch notes should be modified. The stores department should generate pre-numbered goods despatch notes to accompany all goods despatched and copies should be retained for control purposes.

Sales invoices should be prepared and forwarded to customers only after the stores department have confirmed to the sales department that goods have been despatched, by for example forwarding a copy of the pre-numbered despatch note.

Copy invoices should then be forwarded to the accounts department for posting to the accounting records by appropriately experienced employees, who should have no involvement in the receipt of monies from customers.

(viii) Deficiency

The assistant accountant is responsible for dealing with customer invoices queries and the issue of sales credit notes.

Implication

As sales department staff deal with the preparation and processing of sales invoices, it is likely that the assistant accountant will not have the knowledge to deal effectively with customer queries. In addition, the company's exposure to fraud and error is increased as a consequence of the assistant accountant having the discretion to raise credit notes whilst also having authority to post into the company's accounting records.

Recommendations

The assistant accountant should have no involvement in the decision to raise sales credit notes. Customer queries should be directed to individuals involved in the preparation of sales invoices.

(Full marks will be awarded for answers identifying only FOUR deficiencies in the system, for relevant comments as to the implications arising from the deficiency and for making appropriate recommendations).

INVENTORY AND PURCHASING

41 STARLING

The following matters should be covered in the instructions for the physical inventory count of Starling Co as at 31 January 20X5.

(i) There should be adequate supervisory controls, with one individual assuming overall responsibility for the inventory count.

(ii) Employees involved in the inventory count should be independent of those working in the stores and production areas, and counters should work in pairs with one counting inventory and the other recording and checking quantities counted.

(iii) Procedures should ensure that items are marked as 'counted' to avoid the possibility of double counting or omission.

(iv) There should be adequate control over the issue and returning of inventory control sheets, possibly involving the use of pre-numbered sheets with returned sheets being agreed to issued sequences for completeness.

(v) Inventory sheets should be completed in ink and signed by the relevant individuals involved in the counting and recording process.

(vi) Movement of inventory during the count should be prohibited and a special quarantine area should be created in which to store any goods received.

(vii) In order to minimise disruption to the production process, raw materials together with parts and finished goods inventories should be counted first with work-in-progress inventory being counted at the end of the working day.

(viii) There should be stringent controls over cut-off issues with careful note being made of the number of the last goods received, goods returned and goods despatched and raw materials/parts issued notes prior to the inventory count.

(ix) There should be adequate procedures to identify, count and record inventory that is slow moving or obsolete.

42 SMARTBUY

(i) Deficiency

The buyer is responsible for ordering goods, the custody of goods and for the authorisation of invoices when they are received.

Implications

There is a risk of fraud and error due to the involvement of only the buyer in these areas.

Recommendations

To reduce the possibility of fraud and error, the company should ensure that there is proper segregation of duties in the ordering, purchase and custody and recording of inventory.

(ii) Deficiency

Inventory is ordered by telephone.

Implications

There is a risk of unauthorised/wrong goods being ordered and delivered.

Recommendations

The company should introduce a system of documentation to support the ordering process. Purchase orders should be used which are authorised by an independent responsible official of the company. Purchase orders should be pre-printed, pre-numbered and subject to rigid custody controls. The company should also draw up a list of approved suppliers – orders should be placed only with these suppliers unless specific authorisation is obtained to use other suppliers.

(iii) Deficiency

Goods received by the company are not checked for quality.

Implications

Sub-standard goods, defective or damaged goods could be accepted and paid for by the company.

Recommendations

Competent and trained personnel should check all goods received. They should prepare signed goods received notes for each delivery.

Tutorial note

Other weaknesses could be identified in the system described in the question.

43 M

Key answer tips

The key to answering questions on internal control is to apply some common sense and think through the problems that might arise and the ways in which an enterprise might prevent irregularities from creeping into its accounting records.

Requisitions should be authorised by a production manager.

Requisitions should be raised in response to inventory levels reaching predetermined re-order levels.

Orders should be raised by a separate buying department that does not handle inventory or deal with the payment of purchase invoices.

All orders should be on official, pre-numbered order forms. Blank order forms should be kept secure.

Orders should be placed with designated suppliers who have been approved by the head of the buying department.

Any unusual items that cannot be supplied by an approved supplier should be authorised by the head of the buying department.

44 ZED

Deliveries should be made to a designated goods inward area.

Inventory items should be agreed to the details on the delivery note. Any discrepancies or problems with the quality or condition of the inventory should be noted on the delivery note, both on the copy signed as a receipt and on the copy retained by the company.

All valid receipts should be recorded on a pre-numbered goods received note. This should note the date, the description of the goods and the quantity.

Any deliveries not ordered or deliveries that are damaged must be returned to the supplier and not recorded as goods received on a goods received note.

Goods returned to suppliers should be the subject of a formal returns note. This should make it clear that the goods are not being resold, but are being returned. All such despatch notes should be linked to the related debit note issued by the company to the supplier.

PAYROLL

45 PEACH CO

1 Deficiency

The production manager has sole responsibility for recruiting employees to Peach Co.

Implication

The manager may be tempted to introduce non-existent employees into the system leading to the misappropriation of company funds by way of wages payments for non-existent employees.

Recommendation

Employees should be interviewed by the production manager and a responsible personnel official, such that potential employees can be properly identified and vetted prior to employment.

2 Deficiency

Wages clerks, responsible for the processing of wages, have 'amend' access to the wages master file.

Implication

A clerk could be tempted to manipulate data on the wages master file such that they, or their associates are able to benefit from subsequent misappropriation of company funds. For example, a wages clerk could enter details for a non-existent employee or increase the pay rate for a specified employee.

Recommendation

Wages clerks should have only 'read' access to the master file data. New employee details should be entered by a senior responsible official of the company or the wages manager.

3 Deficiency

The wages master file is updated prior to an employee commencing employment with the company.

Implication

There is an increased possibility that unauthorised wages could be paid to employees, prior to commencing employment.

Recommendation

New employee details should be entered on to the master file on a timely basis, after employees have commenced employment with Peach Co.

4 Deficiency

The production manager issues time recording swipe cards to new employees.

Implication

Given the apparent lack of accountability by the production manager over the recruitment of employees, there is an increased likelihood of the misappropriation of company funds by way of wages payments for non-existent employees, such payments would be supported by apparently *bona fide* attendance records.

Recommendation

Stringent controls should be maintained over the issue of swipe cards to employees. Their issue should be controlled by a senior responsible official of the company, independent of the wages and production functions (for example the company accountant) and there should be measures to ensure that cards become operational only when issued.

5 Deficiency

The production manager is able to amend employee details on the time recording unit's master file.

Implication

As with (4) above, the unfettered authority of the production manager to change master file data on the time recording unit adds to the likelihood of fraudulent wages payments being made.

Recommendation

Amendments to data on the master file of the time recording unit should be made only by a senior responsible official of the company, independent of the wages and production functions. The production manager should not have access to master file data.

6 Deficiency

The entry/exit terminals are not monitored.

Implication

Employees' attendance records could be falsified, by for example one individual (arriving on time for work) swiping other late coming employees' cards through a terminal.

Recommendation

Employees' entry/exit terminals should be monitored, or CCTV could be installed, to reduce the temptation to falsify records and thus limit the company's exposure to payments being made for hours not worked.

7 Deficiency

The wages programme does not produce 'exception' reports detailing for example hours worked and payments due outside of expected ranges, or details of starters and leavers in the month.

Implication

Unauthorised payments made as a consequence of unauthorised working patterns or rates of pay may not be recognised. Similarly unauthorised payments to 'starting' or 'leaving' employees may not be recognised.

Recommendation

To facilitate ease of recognition of those payments as described (above), the wages system should be modified or updated to ensure production of monthly exception reports. These should be scrutinised by the wages manager and reviewed by the accountant along with other summaries.

8 Deficiency

The company's bank is instructed to make payments of wages without a prior check of the wages summary by an independent responsible official.

Implication

Notwithstanding other control measures built into the wages system, unauthorised wages payments could still be made by Peach Co. Similarly, as the summaries form the basis of wages posting entries into the company's general ledger, erroneous journal entries could be made into the ledger.

Recommendation

Prior to the closure of the wages programme, all of the monthly summaries produced should be made available to the company's accountant. The accountant should review the summaries and enquire into any abnormal or irregular payments to be made. Queries and apparent discrepancies should be resolved, and updated summaries produced before closure of the wages programme. All final summaries should be signed as checked by the accountant prior to filing.

(**Note:** *Full marks will be awarded for identifying and commenting on any four of the above or other weaknesses in the wages system*)

46 CAFÉS

(a) Four significant matters that would affect the auditor's assessment of inherent risk applying to the wages figure in the case of Cafés are:

(i) The size and geographical spread of the company's activities. With outlets spread across the two regions the auditor may be concerned that payroll input data may go astray in the process of transmission from the outlets to Head Office.

(ii) There is a large number of employees giving rise to a high volume of payroll transactions in each accounting period. This may cause the auditor to be concerned about the scope for errors or omissions in the payroll processing.

(iii) The high rate of staff turnover. Employees joining and leaving give rise to special payroll processing considerations. With a high level of this activity, the auditor may be concerned about the scope for material errors in the processing or in compliance with tax procedures.

(iv) The use of a computer-based accounting system. Auditors involved with such systems will always be concerned about the possible scope for incomplete or inaccurate processing. Specifically in a payroll system, the auditor will have particular concerns about the preservation of the confidentiality of information and the possibility of unauthorised input data or unauthorised changes to standing data such as pay rates.

(b) Control risk is the risk that a material misstatement in an account balance or transaction may not be prevented or detected and corrected by the operation of the entity's accounting and internal control systems. The auditor's assessment of the level of control risk attached to the company's payroll systems will therefore depend on the outcome of the auditor's review and evaluation of those systems.

Part (a) of this answer identified a number of major weaknesses in the controls operated by the company over many aspects of their payroll processing. It is likely therefore that the auditor would be able to place only a limited degree of confidence in the ability of the payroll system to generate complete and accurate payroll output based on authorised input data.

In these circumstances it is likely that the auditor would assess the control risk as being 'high'.

47 RECRUITMENT

Like any asset, they have a value or benefit to being used in the business. In addition, like any other asset, they also have a monetary value. Consequently, there should be control procedures and policies to safeguard the assets, to ensure that any disposal is properly authorised, and to achieve the best possible price upon disposal.

In particular, cars are an attractive asset for thieves to acquire, especially two-year-old executive types of car. They are individually valuable and can be taken away easily – they can simply be driven away. Once the policy has been adopted to dispose of cars when they become two years old, management must institute controls to ensure that the best possible sales price is achieved for each car and that the sales price is actually received.

MANAGEMENT LETTER

48 LAKE FOUNDRY

XYZ & Co
Certified Accountants
1 Lord Street
Bridgeville

A Shore Esq,
Managing Director
Lake Foundry
Bridgeville

6 January 20X8

Dear Sir,

Interim Audit for the year ended 31 March 20X8

(a) In accordance with our normal practice we are writing to you concerning matters arising out of our audit of the accounting records of your company and the systems of internal control. These points were discussed with you at our meeting on 3 January 20X8.

We must stress that our tests were necessarily limited by considerations of cost and time and should not therefore be relied upon to reveal all areas of weakness that may exist. We should appreciate your comments on the deficiencies and recommendations as set out below and suggest that we arrange a meeting at a suitable future date.

(b) **Management controls**

Deficiency	Recommendations
1 The company does not produce monthly management or financial information. Without timely and accurate financial information the company will be unable to direct effectively its planned expansion.	We recommend that monthly management accounts are prepared which provide information on sales, profitability and aged receivables and payables.

Deficiency	Recommendations
2 The company does not prepare budgets or cash flow forecasts against which to monitor its performance. These are important management controls enabling the company to respond to any deviations from budget and to plan its strategy for the future.	We recommend that annual profit forecasts and cash flow forecasts are produced and that the monthly management accounts are compared to these budgets so that appropriate action can be taken immediately if necessary.
3 The pricing policy of the company is inadequate due to the following: • It is informal and cannot be relied upon to be adequately updated. • Loss making products cannot easily be identified. • The lack of financial information means that the overhead recovery rate cannot be monitored.	We recommend that a full and detailed review of the company's costing system is carried out as a matter of urgency. We should be willing to assist in this review if required.
4 The impending retirement of Mr W Shore from the company and the transfer of his shares to Mr A Shore may have both commercial and taxation implications.	We recommend that specialist taxation advice is sought before the transfer of shares is effected. In addition, the loss of Mr W Shore's expertise in the company must be carefully considered and, if necessary, a replacement should be appointed as soon as possible.

(c) Sales and receivables

Deficiency	Recommendations
1 Sales orders are recorded only when the goods have been produced and are ready for despatch. Thus, sales could be omitted or forgotten.	All orders received should be immediately recorded on pre-numbered sales order documents and authorised by Mr A Shore. These pre-numbered documents should comprise a five part set which can be utilised as follows: (1) Sales order – used to initiate production. (2) Delivery note – kept by customer. (3) Delivery note – signed by customer as proof of receipt. (4) Sales invoice – to customer. (5) Sales invoice – retained in accounts department.
2 Sales invoices are not produced until the end of the month of delivery. This could delay the receipt of cash from customers and hence adversely affect the company's liquidity.	Sales invoices should be sent to customers as soon as practical after delivery.

Deficiency	Recommendations
3 Sales orders and invoices are not authorised. Thus errors in pricing etc. could be made or sales made to uncreditworthy customers.	All orders and invoices should be authorised by Mr A Shore.
4 An aged list of receivables is not prepared at the end of each month, nor is a sales ledger control account prepared. Thus, control over the sales ledger is weak and credit control and cash collection is inefficient.	We recommend that a sales ledger control account and aged list of receivables are prepared monthly so that control over receivables and cash collection can be improved.

(d) Purchases and payables

Deficiency	Recommendations
1 There is no formal procedure for the ordering and receipt of goods. Invoices which are unauthorised and for which the goods have not been received could be posted to the ledger.	We recommend that the company introduce a pre-numbered purchase order and goods received note set. Thus, all goods ordered can be formally authorised by Mr A Shore and the goods received note can be checked to the purchase invoice before it is posted to the purchase ledger.
2 A purchase ledger control account and aged list of payables is not produced at the month end. Purchase ledger balances are not checked to suppliers' statements – thus, incorrect amounts could be paid.	We recommend that a purchase ledger control account and aged list of payables are prepared monthly. Purchase ledger balances should be checked to suppliers' statements before payments are made.

We should be happy to discuss any of the above matters in more detail should you require it. Finally, we should like to take this opportunity of thanking you and your staff for your assistance during the course of our interim audit.

Yours faithfully,

A N Accountant

49 VENTAIR

Auditors & Co
Certified Accountants
Longley

The Board of Directors
Ventair

Dear Sirs

Financial Statements for the year ended 30 June 20X0

In accordance with our normal practice we set out in this letter those matters which arose during our recent audit as a result of our review of the accounting systems and procedures operated by your company.

These matters were identified during our normal audit procedures which are designed for the purposes of expressing our opinion on the company's financial statements. Our work did not encompass a detailed examination of all aspects of the system and cannot be relied on necessarily to disclose fraud or other irregularities or to include all possible improvements in internal control.

(i) Segregation of duties:

Deficiency

There is inadequate segregation of duties within the purchasing department as the administration department manager is currently responsible for all key tasks i.e. ordering, recording and payment.

Implications

There is a risk that unauthorised purchases could be made.

Recommendation

The ordering, recording and payment functions should be segregated and different personnel used to perform these tasks.

(ii) Finished goods area:

Deficiency

Finished goods are not currently checked to the customer order prior to being loaded onto the delivery vehicle.

Implications

If the goods delivered do not agree to the customer order Ventair would be unable to confirm whether or not the correct goods were despatched.

Recommendation

A copy of the customer order should be checked to the goods at the time of loading and be signed and dated.

(iii) Payment of production department staff:

Deficiency

Production department staff currently complete their time records manually and these are not checked by the supervisor for accuracy.

Implications

Production department workers could fraudulently or erroneously complete their time records and this could go undetected.

Recommendation

Implementation of a clocking system should be considered and adequate controls should be implemented to ensure that the system operates effectively. At present all-time records should be checked by the production department supervisor.

(iv) Payment of office staff:

Deficiency

Changes to office staff salaries are currently notified verbally to the payroll department.

Implications

Inaccurate/fraudulent amendments could be made to the salary details, and staff subsequently paid inaccurate amounts.

Recommendation

All approved salary changes should be documented by the personnel department and sent to the payroll department.

Our comments have been discussed with the finance director and these matters will be considered in future audits. We look forward to receiving your comments, and any actions to be taken on the above issues. Should you require any further information or explanation do not hesitate to contact us.

This letter has been produced for the sole use of your company. It must not be disclosed to a third party, or quoted or referred to, without our written consent. No responsibility is assumed by us to any other person.

We should like to take this opportunity to thank you and your staff for their assistance and co-operation during the course of the audit.

Yours faithfully

Auditors & Co

EVALUATION TECHNIQUES AND TESTING

50 SHIRTS

Substantive tests that I would want to carry out in respect of payroll in the interim accounts of Shirts are as follows:

(i) reconcile the figure for wages in the interim accounts to the nominal ledger balance(s);

(ii) physically verify the existence of a sample of employees in the payroll to the employee records;

(iii) perform analytical review to identify the reasonableness of the wages figure against previous years and the budget and also consider any known employment changes in the year e.g. redundancies;

(iv) re-perform gross and net wages calculations for a sample of employees against clock cards and other relevant documentation;

(v) test a sample of deductions, both statutory and non-statutory in the payroll to the source documents and relevant employee authorisation, and also to the cash book and nominal ledger;

(vi) test a sample of starters and leavers and ensure that they were only paid for the relevant period and that all relevant documentation has been completed;

(vii) test a sample of gross and net weekly wages totals from the payroll to the nominal ledger and investigate any differences;

(viii) review the amount of the weekly wages totals and investigate any significant variations.

Note: Only FIVE tests were asked for. However, others have been provided for information; also where samples are used in tests it is important that testing is performed in both directions i.e. from source to destination and vice versa.

CONTROLS IN COMPUTER SYSTEMS

51 KOLA

Accountants & Co
Capital City

Mr. T. Simms – Director
Kola
Capital City
6 May 20X8

Dear Mr Simms,

Following our recent discussions I consider it appropriate to clarify a few matters regarding our audit approach for the year ending 31 December 20X8 to ensure there is no misunderstanding.

I am sure you can appreciate that audit planning is always an important part of any audit, but especially so when computers are used by clients. The reasons for this are as follows:

(i) Inappropriate systems

In many instances the introduction of a PC based system is carried out without adequate thought as to the precise requirements:

- there will probably be no formal feasibility study;
- there will have been no systems analysis;
- there will generally be no formal specification for the system.

PC-based software is generally not specific to any one type of business, and thus there is a danger that the system is inappropriate.

In this situation, there is no suggestion of the auditors having been involved in the introduction of the system, although the advice received from your friend is at least a small measure of feasibility check.

(ii) Poor introduction

PCs are often introduced in a fairly relaxed manner without, for instance, a proper balancing off of the manual records, or without a parallel run. In this instance the control account imbalance may well be carried forward from the old system, and without any parallel run it is difficult to establish where the fault lies.

(iii) Poor day-to-day operations

PC-based systems are typically introduced without the rigours of staff training, operator manuals and post implementation reviews. In this instance there is no evidence of these steps having been undertaken, and again the control account problem may well be symptomatic of accounting problems.

(iv) Weak internal controls

PC-based systems do not generally have formal internal controls:

- the PC is typically in an open office, with free access to staff
- arrangements for backing up and storage of backup tapes/discs are usually ad hoc
- controls over operators, like segregation of duties and passwords, are generally inadequate.

In the circumstances of Kola many of the above observations are apparent:

- the machine is available for all staff
- the password is unprotected
- backing up is inadequate
- no printouts of standing data amendments are obtained.

All of these features require the auditor to amend his plan so that there is a greater emphasis on substantive testing.

If you have any queries on this matter please do not hesitate to contact me.

Yours sincerely

K Janeway

Audit Partner

52 OILCO

Questions to ask accountant to enable evaluation of controls over sales and receivables

In these questions documents relate to sales invoices, cash receipts and credit notes issued to customers.

(i) Are there controls to ensure that all documents are input to the computer system (i.e. numeric sequence checks or batch totals)? Give examples of these controls.

(ii) What controls are there to ensure that documents are accurately input to the computer system? (Verification on-screen and detailed computer validation checks.)

(iii) Are all documents signed by a responsible official to authorise them before they are input to the computer? This particularly applies to sales invoices.

(iv) Are controls over processing on the computer adequate to ensure that all documents are completely and accurately processed (i.e. run-to-run totals and agreement of output with input)? Give examples of these controls.

(v) What controls are there to ensure that all the output is received from the computer system, and that this output is correctly handled? (Agreement of input to output by input/output controllers.)

(vi) How are changes to the master file authorised? Does a responsible official authorise the creation of any new receivables ledger account, and the writing-off of any old accounts as irrecoverable debts?

53 SOMETECH

(a) (i) Application controls are those controls which relate to transactions and master file/standing data in an accounting system which relate to the specific computer based application. These controls can be programmed i.e. contained within the application code itself or manual and they exist to ensure that the accounting records are complete and accurate and any transactions processed to update the records are valid.

(ii) General controls are all those controls which relate to the environment in which the applications operate and relate to all those applications from the development to the operational stage. General controls can also be manual or programmed and exist to ensure that all applications are properly developed and maintained, and operated within a controlled environment that ensures all program and data files are complete, accurate and valid.

It is important that both application and general controls are strong within any organisation as weak general controls can undermine strong application controls.

(b) Parallel running of two computer systems i.e. the old system and the new system prior to solely using the new system, is a common technique that is used to ensure that the new system is operating satisfactorily, and that all information produced is complete and accurate, prior to discontinuing the use of the old system. Clearly the directors would not want to transfer over to the new system unless they are confident that all information is being accurately processed and that information can be produced on a timely basis and can be relied upon. During the period of parallel run, identical information would be produced from both systems and compared to ensure that both are identical; in the event that any differences were found these should be investigated and corrected prior to discontinuing use of the old system.

As auditor I would want to be involved during this period to facilitate the timely examination and testing of the controls within the new system. Furthermore I would review the output from both systems and compare the two to ensure their accuracy. I would also want to review the procedures (and test compliance with those procedures) operated by the organisation's staff to test the accuracy of the new system. In the event that I found any errors or encountered problems with the data or procedures I would want to make relevant recommendations to management.

54 SEMI

(a) The speed of recording transactions will be unaffected in one sense, but should increase in another. The scenario suggests that it will still be a full time task for the bookkeeper to input transactions after the new system has been implemented. That suggests that it will not have a significant effect on the time taken to enter any given transaction into the system. The one big change is that the computerised system will dispense with the need to maintain daybooks and that means that each transaction will update the key files immediately after it is input. Under the existing system the nominal and personal ledgers will only be updated after the daybook information has been carried over and that might happen only once a month.

The new system should make it possible to generate trial balances and basic accounting statements on a monthly basis. It should also be possible to produce detailed aged analyses of receivables and payables and that might enable management to manage cash more effectively.

(b) Areas of concern

(i) Opening balances might be carried over incorrectly. That could mean that payables are overpaid or that receivables receive understated statements.

(ii) Standing information, such as addresses, might be incorrect. That could involve cheques being sent to the wrong addresses or customers receiving the wrong rate of discount.

(iii) Staff could use the confusion associated with the changeover to make fraudulent changes, e.g. by creating a fictitious supplier.

(iv) The system might not have the necessary facilities to meet the company's needs (e.g. the ability to handle foreign currency transactions associated with imports).

(v) The system could be accessible to any member of staff when the bookkeeper is not using it and that could leave the system more open to fraud.

(vi) The data files might become corrupted, leaving the company without important accounting data.

55 FOZZ

When planning any audit assignment consideration needs to be given to the timing of the audit and the approach to the audit procedures which will be carried out. The auditors should therefore establish at an early stage what effect the introduction of the computer-based accounting system will have on the timing of the audit work and on the manner in which they will need to perform their audit work.

An important part of the planning process in this context will be to ensure the availability of audit staff with an appropriate level of specialist knowledge and experience in auditing the computer-based accounting system. Manufacturing environments, such as that likely to be encountered here, tend to give rise to complex accounting issues, even for sophisticated computer based systems. The auditors may well see this as generating a high level of inherent risk on the audit, which, as usual, needs to be reflected in the planning process.

In addition, consideration will need to be given to the use of Computer Assisted Audit Techniques (CAATs) in order to obtain appropriate audit evidence and to increase the efficiency of the audit. The auditors of Fozz may need to consider purchasing or developing new computer programs to examine the contents of the computer files of the company, if appropriate software is not currently available to them.

Finally the time scale for the implementation of the new system may affect the approach to audit planning. If the implementation date is part way through the accounting period then the auditors will need to carry out audit tests covering the periods both before and after the implementation date. Similarly the auditors will need to gain evidence that account balances were completely and accurately transferred to the new system.

AUDIT EVIDENCE (INCLUDING COMPUTER-BASED SYSTEMS) AND SAMPLING

GENERAL PRINCIPLES

56 AUDIT EVIDENCE I

(a) **Types of audit evidence**

(i) **Auditor-originated evidence**

Evidence originated by the auditor is more reliable than evidence from any other source. This is certainly the case because it is very unlikely that the auditor-originated evidence will be manipulated in any way, whereas other sources of evidence are more likely to be manipulated to accord with management's wishes.

Auditor-originated evidence is therefore of the highest quality, and the auditor will place great reliance on this.

Examples of auditor-originated evidence include:

1. Analytical review of the company's accounts. The auditor will review the financial statements to ensure that they agree with his other knowledge of the business. He may also compute other ratios and statistics to assist him in this analysis.

2. Observation of the company's accounting system to ensure that the control system is operating as described by management. Although this evidence is limited because employees may amend their work practices when they note that they are being observed, it does serve to check the basic accuracy of the recorded system.

3. Inspection of the company's assets to ensure that they exist. This test, however, gives no indication by itself of ownership or the value of the assets.

4. Agreeing the accuracy of the client's records by using arithmetical checks. The basic accuracy of the salary expense at a company, for example, can be checked by multiplying the average number of employees for the year by the average wage rate.

(ii) **Evidence created by third parties**

Evidence obtained from independent sources outside the enterprise is more reliable than that secured solely from within the enterprise. This evidence is thus normally reliable and may contradict management evidence. For this reason the evidence should be addressed directly to the auditor to ensure that it is not suppressed by management.

The value of the evidence is weakened slightly because the auditor cannot observe its production and therefore cannot tell diligently prepared evidence from mere guesses.

Examples of third party evidence include:

1 Bank letter, receivables' circularisations and other situations where the auditor requests evidence from a third party. As long as the replies are returned directly to the auditor they are considered reliable and a good check on the company's accounting system. Thus if the company had inflated sales at the end of the year by debiting receivables and crediting sales with dummy sales invoices, the debtor would be unlikely to agree to the overstated balance on this account.

2 Other evidence issued not directly to the auditor but which he will use e.g. purchase invoices. The auditor would always expect these to be available in their original form and if substituted in any way, would be put on enquiry until the reason for this was found.

3 Other documents issued by third parties, but not directly for any individual's use e.g. price lists. These can be used to agree the accuracy of purchase invoices or, in some cases, to assist in net realisable value calculations where the company's own evidence is lacking (e.g. lack of after-date sales invoices).

(iii) **Evidence created by the management of the client**

Management may be under pressure to distort the financial statements e.g. to meet the expectations put on a company as a result of a profit forecast or to hide their own fraudulent activities. On any audit, therefore, the auditor must try and make a judgement on how reliable he thinks the management evidence will be and set his testing levels accordingly.

The auditor is unlikely to place the same amount of reliance on management evidence as on either his own or third party evidence because of the inherent bias mentioned above. Nevertheless, it is important that, where management evidence is to be relied upon, this is obtained in writing as written evidence is more reliable than oral evidence.

Examples of management evidence include:

1 Letter of representation. This is a letter addressed to the auditor concerning material decisions made by management in the production of the financial statements. The statements in this letter should always be supported by other corroborative evidence, but it remains a crucial form of evidence at the completion of any audit.

2 Discussions with management during the audit concerning the internal control system. The auditor may note potential weaknesses in the system and will therefore need management's comments as to the accuracy of this information.

3 Evidence regarding other auditor queries raised e.g. problems with the financial statements. The auditor may disagree with, say, the depreciation rate of a particular class of asset. He will therefore need management's comments on this.

(b) Considerations in evaluating audit evidence

(i) Sufficiency of evidence

There is no hard and fast rule concerning the precise amount of evidence that the auditor must collect for each audit area. The auditor must use his own skill and judgement to decide how many items to test, for example, in his main sales test. The knowledge of the business, the degree of risk associated with the test, and the reliability of the evidence collected will assist in the decision. For each client, however, the decision must be made. The consideration here, then, is that each client is different, and that no standard testing quantity can be applied to all clients; the auditor must always use his own skill and judgement to decide the appropriate testing level.

(ii) Relevance of evidence

The evidence collected should not be used to draw conclusions about a testing objective not covered by that test. Thus, merely because a non-current asset register correctly adds up does not mean that all the individual assets actually exist, or that they are correctly valued. The auditor must always ensure that the correct tests are used for the audit objective under consideration.

(iii) Degree of knowledge

In some situations the auditor may have the evidence available to him but he may not be able to evaluate this properly. For example, at a jewellery store he may not be able to value the inventory correctly. In this case specialist advice should be sought. Similarly, the auditor may not understand the evidence as in the case of some legal contracts, and here a solicitor may be needed to explain fully the effect of the contract on the client.

57 AUDIT EVIDENCE II

(a) Audit evidence is simply material collected and recorded by the auditor in order to support the opinion expressed in the audit report.

(b) There are inherent limitations to much of the evidence collected by the auditor. Management must make a variety of estimates and assumptions and these can have material effects on the financial statements. It is possible to gather evidence to establish that the adjustments are reasonable, but this may not be conclusive.

The auditor must complete the audit in a reasonable time and within a reasonable cost. There is little point in publishing highly accurate figures which are too late to be of any use to the shareholders and other users. Similarly, there is little point in providing a service that is so expensive that nobody can afford to use it. This does not mean that the auditor will be unable to collect sufficient evidence, but it may mean that the evidence gathered is less persuasive than would be the case given unlimited resources.

(c) Inspection, observation, enquiry and confirmation and analytical procedures

ANSWERS TO PRACTICE QUESTIONS : SECTION 4

58 AUDIT EVIDENCE III

Inspection of records involves looking at a piece of documentary evidence in order to ensure that the details support an entry in the financial statements.

The auditor might inspect an invoice in order to prove that a purchase recorded in the accounts actually took place.

The auditor might inspect a signature on a document to ensure that a transaction had been authorised by the appropriate member of staff.

Observation involves looking at a process or procedure being performed by others.

The auditor might attend the year-end inventory count to observe the procedures carried out by the company's staff.

The auditor might observe the process of opening mail in order to ensure that the control procedures laid down in the company's procedures manual are being followed.

Recalculation involves checking the accuracy of calculations on documents or in accounting records.

The auditor might check that the casts and extensions on a purchase invoice are all correct, either to provide some support for the entry in the purchases account or to provide some assurance that this calculation had been checked by the company as part of its control procedures.

The auditor might check the total of an account balance, either to support an entry in the financial statements or as a compliance test to ensure that the program that calculated the total was written and operating correctly.

Analytical procedures involve reviewing the figures in the financial statements to ensure that they are reasonable.

The auditor might calculate the gross profit percentage and compare it with the previous year. Any discrepancy could indicate a problem with the recording of sales or purchases or with the inventory count.

The auditor might check the total for depreciation by proof in total. This would involve multiplying the book value before depreciation by the depreciation rate and comparing this with the recorded figure.

59 AUDIT EVIDENCE IV

(i) **Observation**

Consists of looking at a process or procedure performed by others.

Example – the observation of the opening of the mail of an entity to ensure that at least two employees are present to receive and witness the receipt of monies received by the entity.

(ii) **Recalculation**

Consists of checking the arithmetical accuracy of source documents and accounting records or of performing independent calculations. It may be performed manually or electronically.

Example – checking the accuracy of extensions of inventory calculations to verify the accuracy of the valuation of reported inventory.

(**Note**: Full marks will be awarded for providing the same or similar explanations and examples to those above.)

FAU: FOUNDATIONS IN AUDIT

60 EMPLOYMENT AS A JUNIOR AUDITOR

Note: Only THREE procedures were required by the question.

An auditor may use the following procedures (in addition to enquiry and confirmation) to obtain audit evidence:

- **Inspection** consists of examining accounting records, documents or assets.

    Example – An auditor may verify the existence of a tangible asset (for example a computer) by using this procedure.

- **Observation** consists of looking at a process or a procedure being performed by others.

    Example – An auditor may obtain evidence of the accuracy of inventory count procedures by observing the inventory count being carried out.

- **Computation** consists of checking the arithmetical accuracy of documents and accounting records or performing independent calculations of figures which are reflected in the financial statements.

    Example – An auditor may obtain evidence of the accuracy of a reported figure for depreciation of tangible non-current assets by calculating the depreciation for the period on the basis of the company's accounting policy and comparing the figure with that recorded by the client.

- **Analytical procedures** consist of the analysis of relationships between items of financial data, or between items of financial data and non-financial data from the same or different periods for a given enterprise, or comparing data between two or more enterprises.

    Example – An auditor may obtain audit evidence as to the reasonableness of a reported figure for accrued payroll costs by checking the calculation of the reported figure and comparing it with that of the previous period. Any major differences should be investigated.

INVENTORY

61 DIAMOND

Tests that could be performed to ensure that the net realisable value of the inventory is correct include:

(i) Compare current year results with prior years i.e. profit margins, sales revenues and inventory turnover and investigate any significant differences.

(ii) Consider any changes that have occurred within the last year which could affect inventory valuations (e.g. new fashions, technological developments).

(iii) Compare selling prices to those charged by competitors (if prices elsewhere are lower this could affect Diamond's inventory value).

(iv) Compare the valuation of a sample of inventory lines this year to last year's valuations; if after taking into account the effects of inflation there is little difference then this is likely to indicate the accuracy of the valuation.

(v) Check a sample of sale prices as soon after the year end as possible to ensure that prices were not artificially high at the year end.

(vi) Review trade magazines and relevant publications to identify any changes within the industry which could indicate poor/reduced demand levels.

62 EMERALD

The main reasons for the auditor's attendance at the inventory count are:

(i) to verify existence by tracing items on the inventory listings to the physical inventory,

(ii) to verify completeness by tracing items of inventory to the inventory listings provided by the client,

(iii) to identify obsolete, slow moving and damaged inventories by reviewing the actual inventory that appear to be old or damaged,

(iv) to verify controls such as proper security by reviewing the company premises to ensure that appropriate controls are in place,

(v) to ensure that there is proper cut off (i.e. that sales before the year end are included within the current year's sales, and that all items included in the inventory figure have not been sold at the year-end) by ensuring that inventory movement is limited during the inventory count,

(vi) to ensure that client staff are counting the inventory in accordance with the client's count instructions to ensure that the count is complete and accurate by observing staff during the count.

As inventory is a material item, the auditor would expect to attend the count at each location. Ideally, as jewellery is highly valuable and easily transportable, the client should hold the count at the same time in each location, with a member of the audit team in attendance at each location.

63 COACHES

(i) The reasons for giving particular audit attention to goods received notes, maintenance job cards and goods returned notes issued both immediately prior to and after the year-end inventory count are primarily due to 'cut off'. If there are no proper cut off procedures it is possible that the company's accounting records are inaccurate and do not properly reflect the actual inventory transactions of the period. If errors existed, these could be as follows:

- the indebtedness of the company to suppliers could be inaccurate if goods returned notes are recorded in the wrong period;
- payables could be over or under stated as amounts recorded on the goods received notes may be included in the wrong period;
- the maintenance costs in the company's accounting records could be over or under stated.

(ii) The last goods received note, maintenance job card and goods returned note issued immediately prior to the inventory count would be recorded at the time of the inventory count. These should then be traced through the accounting records to ensure that these have been recorded in the correct period. Following this, I would also record the first goods received note, maintenance job card and goods returned notes issued immediately after the inventory count and ensure that these have been accurately recorded in the correct period.

It is also important that work in progress is considered and the maintenance job cards should be examined to identify all such jobs at the year end date to ensure that the cut off procedures have operated effectively.

64 SWEET SCENTS

(a) Statement 1

The financial director's statement is not valid. He has misunderstood the respective roles of the employees and the auditor at the inventory count. It is the employees' responsibility to accurately count the inventory and then to value it at the lower of cost and net realisable value. The directors of the company are responsible for preparing financial statements that give a true and fair view, including giving a fair valuation to inventory held.

The auditor's responsibility is to give an opinion on whether the financial statements give a true and fair view. His attendance at the inventory count is to gather evidence on whether he can state that the inventory figure is fair. He will observe the employees carrying out the count and make very limited test counts to check the employees' work. The auditor is certainly not responsible for the accuracy of the inventories figure. His attendance at the count is to observe the employees as they conduct their procedures 'to carry out a thorough count and valuation of all inventories', as the financial director has put it.

(b) Statement 2

The auditors must be concerned that the descriptions given on the outside of the boxes may not truly represent what is inside the box. Neither the auditors nor the employees should unreservedly accept the description given on each box. It would be possible for a box to state that it contained 1,000 objects at a cost of $1 each. The company would feel foolish if it paid $1,000 but discovered some months later that it had bought an empty box.

At the inventory count the company must open some of the boxes and confirm that the contents are as they are described on the outside of the box. This confirmation should cover both description of the items and their quantities. Since the items also have 'use by' dates, it is clear that they have a finite life. When looking inside the boxes, the company should check that items prior to their stated 'use by' dates still look usable. If a box claims to contain 1kg of rose petals that have a 'use by' date in two months' time, but the petals are mouldy and rotten, then the company should note this fact for future consideration in valuing the inventory.

Statement 3

The auditors should be concerned that all inventories held at 30 June 20X5 are valued at the lower of cost and net realisable value (NRV). If NRV is lower than cost, as with the flood-damaged items, then it would be wrong to value them at cost. They must be written down to NRV.

At the inventory count, the company must identify all items for which NRV might be lower than cost. This would include damaged items (such as after the flood in May 20X5), obsolete items (such as items no longer in fashion) and items deliberately sold at a loss (loss leaders to attract sales of other items). When the company comes to value the inventory counted at the count, such items must be written down to NRV if this is estimated to be below cost.

Statement 4

The Fleurs Bleu products are worthless so have an NRV of zero. They are currently in inventory, so the auditors will want to ensure that they are correctly valued at the lower of cost and NRV, i.e. at zero. They must all be written off to zero now, in the year ending 30 June 20X5, not next year. The date when they are physically thrown out is irrelevant; the loss is foreseeable now so must be recognised now.

At the inventory count, the company should ensure that all the Fleurs Bleu inventory is identified separately. It represents 5% of the total value of inventory, so there could be a lot of it. In the valuation process, this entire line of products must be valued at nil.

65 JEANS

(i) Inherent risk can be defined as the susceptibility of an account balance or class of transactions to misstatement that could be material, individually or when aggregated with misstatements in other balances or classes, assuming that there were no related internal controls.

(ii) There are several factors associated with the audit of the area of the inventory of Jeans as at 31 July 20X3, which would lead inherent risk to be assessed as 'high'. These can be conveniently grouped under the headings of quantity and valuation as follows:

Quantity

The company has significant amounts of raw materials, consumables and work in progress inventory at its factory base. It also has significant amounts of finished goods held at a separate warehouse and by (third party) outlets.

There are inevitable difficulties associated with the quantification of these items of inventory. In particular, difficulties often occur in the quantification of partly used supplies of raw materials and consumable inventory and in the quantification of the amount of work in progress at various stages of the manufacturing process. In assessing quantities, subjective judgement is often used.

With regard to the finished goods inventory, I would be aware of likely problems in quantifying the amount of inventory at the company's warehouse. I would also be aware of the desirable nature of specific inventory items and their susceptibility to loss, or misappropriation by company staff. However, I would be particularly concerned as to the determination of quantities of inventory held under the company's sale or return system, by third parties and the possibility of misrepresentation in this regard.

Valuation

As the company is engaged in the activity of manufacturing the risk of incorrect valuation being placed on inventory would be inherently high. The amount at which inventory should be stated in the financial statements of Jeans is the total of the lower of cost and the net realisable value of the separate items of inventory or groups of similar items.

Owing to the high volume and nature of inventory items and lines held by a manufacturing company of this type, there are inevitable problems associated with the valuation process. These include such tasks as the identification and valuation of slow moving/out of fashion inventory lines.

Given that in the financial statements of the previous year, quantities of inventory were stated at net realisable value, I would be aware of the risk that inventory at cost in the financial statements for the year ended 31 July 20X3, could be overvalued.

NON-CURRENT ASSETS

66 ANDREW MANUFACTURING

Client:	Andrew Manufacturing	W/P Ref:	E1/1
Y/E Date:	30 September 20X4	Prepared by:	RRT
		Date:	16 August 20X4
		Reviewed by:	GL
		Date:	21 August 20X4

Audit Programme: Non-current assets

Objective: To verify the accuracy of the amounts stated in the financial statements for non-current assets

	W/P Ref	Performed by	Reviewed by
Test			
(i) Obtain from the client a schedule of movements in non-current assets for the year, check the additions on the schedule, agree the totals to the amounts in the draft accounts and the closing balances to the nominal ledger.			
(ii) Check the opening balances on the schedule and in the draft accounts to: • the closing balances in the preceding years accounts; and • closing balances in the underlying books and records for the preceding period.			
(iii) Vouch additions to the non-current assets to purchase invoices or lease agreements, and the entry in the nominal ledger. Also, check that the item has been included in the non-current asset register. Check disposals to supporting documentation (e.g. sales invoice or cash book) and consider whether the disposal proceeds are reasonable. Check the cost and depreciation provision at the date of disposal to the non-current asset register and check that this has been properly deducted on the schedule (in (i) above) and in the nominal ledger. Check that the profit or loss on disposal of the asset has been correctly treated in the nominal ledger.			
(iv) Check the additions of cost, depreciation provision and depreciation charge of the individual non-current assets in the non-current asset register to the amounts on the schedule, draft accounts and nominal ledger.			

(v) Physically inspect a sample of non-current assets. The check should be performed from both the non-current asset register to the non-current assets (which checks that the non-current assets in the register exist) and from the non-current asset to the non-current asset register (which checks that the non-current assets which exist are included in the non-current asset register, and hence in the accounts i.e. complete). In verifying non-current assets, it is important to check the serial number on the item (or vehicle registration number). However, this is not possible for most fixtures and fittings, so only agreement of the description is possible.

If some of the vehicles are located in other parts of the country, obtain a certificate of existence signed by the user of the vehicle (e.g. for salesmen's cars).

(vi) Check that the depreciation rates are reasonable. If there are losses on sale of non-current assets, it is an indication that depreciation rates are inadequate. If there are profits on the sale of non-current assets or a significant proportion of the non-current assets are fully written off, then it is an indication that depreciation rates are too high. However, auditors are more likely to accept too high a depreciation rate than too low a depreciation rate, as they would argue this is a prudent approach.

Non-current assets may become obsolete (e.g. a depreciation rate of 10% on cost would be unrealistic for portable computers).

The auditor would consider whether the remaining lives of the existing non-current assets are realistic by asking the company's senior management and looking at the condition of the non-current assets.

(vii) Consider whether there are any obsolete or unused non-current assets, by asking management, inspecting the minutes of board and management meetings and looking at the non-current assets in the factory. Obsolete non-current assets should be written down to estimated disposal value, and the auditor would consider whether unused non-current assets will be used again – if they are unlikely to be used again, they should be treated in the same way as obsolete non-current assets. By the term 'obsolete' the auditor would mean assets which are of no more economic value to the company – a computer may be technically obsolete, but if it is still used for processing accounting data (or other tasks), it is not 'obsolete' in terms of the discussion above.

(viii) Inspect vehicle registration documents for motor vehicles. Check them to the non-current assets register. The vehicle registration document is not a document of title, but it is good evidence of the existence of the vehicle and that the company may own it.

(ix) Inspect the deeds of the property – the latest conveyance should be in the name of the company. Also the auditor could check with the land registry that the land is registered in the company's name.

(x) Based on the above audit work, the auditor would then decide whether non-current assets as stated in the accounts are satisfactorily stated or not.

RECEIVABLES

67 ASKWITH

(a) **Explanations to the junior auditor**

- If a reply is not received from the initial circularisation letter, a second request should be sent. If a reply is not received from this second request then the debtors should be contacted by telephone. It is important that the client's permission is obtained prior to any direct contact.

- If direct confirmation is not possible or successful, the following procedures should be used:

    (i) review cash received after the year-end to see if the balances have been cleared

    (ii) agree individual outstanding invoices to independent evidence such as delivery notes signed by the customer

    (iii) review credit notes issued after the year-end to ensure receivables should not be reduced

    (iv) review make-up of receivables balance and ensure that it consists of recent invoices

    (v) check authorisation for any unusual entries (journals, contras) in the accounts.

(b)

Client:	Askwith	W/P Ref:	E1/1
Y/E Date:	30 June X8	Prepared by:	RRT
		Date:	16 May 20X8
		Reviewed by:	GL
		Date:	21 May 20X8
Audit Programme:	Cut off (Receivables)		

	W/P Ref	Performed by	Reviewed by
(i) Agree a sample of despatch notes, from either side of the year-end, to invoices to ensure that the dates agree (details of the last despatch notes would usually be taken at the inventory count).			
(ii) Review credit notes issued after the year-end and check that they do not relate to inventory returned before the year-end etc.			
(iii) Check that cash received has been allocated to the correct period.			

CASH

68 BON VOYAGE

Client: Bon Voyage   W/P Ref:
Y/E Date: 30 November 20X5   Prepared by:
                                          Date:
                                          Reviewed by:
                                          Date:

Audit Evidence – Bank and Cash

To assist you with the conduct of the audit I have provided the following guidance for the above items – please insert this paper in the planning section of the current audit file.

The following evidence is required with respect to the bank balance and bank loans:

1   Re-perform the year-end bank reconciliation and review or re-perform earlier period-ends' reconciliations and trace a sample of reconciling items to post year end bank statements.

2   Ensure cut-off is correct by reviewing transactions either side of the year-end for major transactions – any large receipts or payments should be vouched to ensure that they have been recorded in the correct accounting period.

3   Obtain a bank letter as third party confirmation for the year-end balances, etc.

4   Check that any accounts opened or closed during the year were authorised.

5   Note any rights of set-off or other special terms.

6   Confirm details of any security given for the loan, and ensure disclosure is adequate.

7   Vouch interest rates, terms of loan, etc., to loan agreement.

8   Check that loan repayments to be made within one year are correctly disclosed as current liabilities.

Evidence required in respect of cash balances is:

1   Review system for ensuring security of travellers' cheques and cash.

2   Count cash and travellers' cheques at year-end (auditor should attend a sample of such counts, in teams of two, and in the presence of client staff).

LIABILITIES AND OTHER ITEMS

69 PEAR CO

Examples of audit tests that should be carried out include the following:

Trade Payables

(i) Agree reported trade payables values to trade payables control account reconciliation and underlying working papers/schedules.

(ii) Carry out analytical procedures and make enquiries as appropriate, ensuring that 54% increase on previous year balance makes sense taking all matters into account.

(iii) Check reconciliation of supplier account statements to trade payable ledger balances, prepared by Pear Co staff. Enquire into any abnormalities and carry out further reconciliations as required.

(iv) Review cut-off procedures for goods received and recognition of amounts payable at 30 April 20X8. Test to ensure accuracy.

(v) Review unmatched goods received notes (goods received but associated invoice not received at 30 April 20X8), and ensure inclusion in trade payables value.

(vi) Review trade payables control account postings immediately, prior to and post 30 April 20X8 and enquire into veracity of unusual items.

(vii) Use CAATs as appropriate to identify for further investigation, long outstanding balances including those with no recent activity and accounts containing unusual debit entries.

70 APPLE CO

Examples of audit tests that should be carried out include the following:

Provision

(i) Read relevant correspondence (including legal correspondence) relating to the damages claim and compare the value of the claim as reported in the statement of profit or loss to underlying estimates and opinions available.

(ii) Discuss the nature and amount of the claim with the responsible officials of the client, and enquire as to underlying rationale of the sum provided. If appropriate, with client permission, seek confirmation of the value of claim from an independent expert.

(iii) Examine the minutes of board or management meetings to obtain substantiating evidence as to the existence and nature of the claim.

(iv) Scrutinise appropriate expense accounts to identify expenditure already incurred in connection with the claim and costs possibly duplicated in the final provision.

(v) Obtain permission from the directors of Apple Co and write to the company legal advisers to confirm the likelihood of Apple Co having to settle the claim and the likely value of the claim.

(vi) Check disclosure of the provision in the financial statements in accordance with relevant international financial reporting standards.

71 FARRINGTON

Client: Farrington	W/P Ref: E1/1
Y/E Date: 31 October 20X5	Prepared by: RRT
	Date: 20 October 20X5
	Reviewed by: GL
	Date: 20 October 20X5
Audit Programme: Trade payables	

	W/P Ref	Performed by	Reviewed by
(i) Obtain a schedule of trade payables analysed by age. Reconcile to general ledger control account and check casts.			
(ii) Circularise a sample of payables and fully investigate any reconciling items.			
(iii) Perform cut-off tests between purchases and inventories.			
(iv) Carry out analytical reviews e.g. purchases month by month, payables' days, etc.			
(v) Review a sample of supplier statement reconciliations and investigate any differences.			

72 OXTON WHOLESALERS

Procedures:

(i) Obtain a list of trade payables and agree total to the control account in the nominal ledger. The addition of the listing would be checked.

(ii) Reconcile a sample of X payables' balances to suppliers' statements.

(iii) For balances where a statement is not available consider a payables' circularisation. This should include nil balances.

(iv) Check cut off by reference to the last goods received note number before the year end (noted at inventory count attendance). Working backwards from that number ensure that invoices have been received for all those deliveries and are correctly included in purchases for that period or, if not, that appropriate accruals have been made.

(v) Compare the list of accruals with previous years and investigate any unusual changes.

(vi) Enquire of management whether all material accruals have been included. For example, the company may have contracted to buy some new fixtures and fittings which should possibly be included in the accounts if delivery is awaited. It may also be appropriate to write to the company's solicitors enquiring if there are any legal matters pending for which an accrual or provision should be made.

73 CLOTHING

Procedures:

(i) Select a sample of potential balances to confirm by sampling from the debits to the purchases account or payments made during the year.

(ii) For selected suppliers, write and ask for direct confirmation of the amount due as at the confirmation date.

(iii) Reconcile responses to the suppliers' confirmation. The timing differences should be checked back to supporting documentation to ensure that there is a valid reason for the discrepancy.

(iv) Post verified balances to the payables listing which forms the basis of the figure in the statement of financial position. Cast the schedule of balances.

(v) Check cut-off at the year-end by checking the date of any large payments recorded during the week before the year-end and by ensuring that any large receipts of goods have either been included in year-end payables or the purchases accrual.

SAMPLING

74 AUDIT SAMPLING

(i) **Haphazard selection**

This is a method of selection in which the auditor attempts to ensure that all items in a population have the same statistical probability of being selected by choosing items haphazardly.

(ii) **Systematic selection**

This is a method of selection in which the auditor selects items using a constant interval between selections. The first item may be selected on a random or haphazard basis, and thereafter the sampling interval is derived by the auditor, for example, by dividing the population by the sample size.

75 CROMWELL

Client:	Cromwell	W/P Ref:	G1/1
Y/E Date:	31 March 20X7	Prepared by:	RRT
		Date:	6 January 20X7
		Reviewed by:	GL
		Date:	10 January 20X7

Main factors which determine sample sizes when performing substantive testing:

(i) **Assurance required**

Based on an assessment of the level of inherent risk and control risk, the auditor will determine the level of detection risk he can accept consistent with the need to manage overall audit risk to an acceptable level. The level of detection risk is the converse of the assurance required from detailed substantive testing. Thus a level of assurance of say 90% will require larger samples than a level of 50%.

(ii) Tolerable error

Tolerable error is the level of error within a population that can be reached and still leave the auditor with sufficient assurance about his audit objective. Whilst not the same as materiality, it is closely related to materiality – materiality is an overall measure for the financial statements as a whole, whereas tolerable misstatement is a subset of materiality related to individual financial statement areas. As the tolerable error increases, the sample size decreases.

(iii) Expected error

Where the auditor expects a higher than normal error rate (either from past experience of this client or because the client has alerted us to this possibility) the auditor will compensate for this by increasing his sample size.

(iv) Extent of stratification possible

Where the facility exists to obtain a stratified listing of a population, this enables the auditor to deliberately bias his sample towards the higher value items. In this way it is often possible to target a high proportion of the value of the population whilst examining relatively few items. Clearly, if the extent to which stratification is possible improves, the sample sizes would be expected to reduce.

AUDIT COMPLETION

76 REVIEW AND REPORTING

'Hot' Review

This type of review involves any review of audit work carried out, prior to the signing of the audit report.

Work may be reviewed as and when it is being carried out by audit staff, during the course of the audit, by a more experienced member of staff. In such circumstances a good review should ensure that adequate feedback is given to the individual(s) carrying out the work thus enabling them to make good any omissions in the procedures they have carried out.

In any event all work carried out should be reviewed at the final stage of the audit, by the partner responsible for the audit assignment. A thorough review at this stage should ensure that the audit work is reviewed alongside the financial statements, that any risk areas identified during the audit process have been adequately covered by the audit work carried out, and that all conclusions have been properly stated and are adequately supported.

'Cold' Review

This type of review involves any type of review carried out after the audit has been completed, by persons who are independent of it. Such a review may be carried out either internally or externally.

An internal review may be carried out by suitably qualified staff, from the same office or perhaps from another office of the same firm. Alternatively, it may be carried out by another audit firm (a 'peer review'). In either case a good review should ensure that adequate feedback is given so that perceived weaknesses in procedures, may be discussed and improved where deemed appropriate.

ANSWERS TO PRACTICE QUESTIONS : SECTION 4

77 AUDITORS' OPINION

It would be appropriate for auditors to modify their report on the audited financial statements of a limited company in the following circumstances:

Where the auditor is unable to obtain sufficient appropriate audit evidence to conclude that the financial statements as a whole are free from material misstatement (i.e. where there is a limitation on the scope of the audit.)

(i) Qualified opinion – where the effect of the subject matter on the financial statements is material but not pervasive

(ii) Disclaimer of opinion – where the effect of the subject matter on the financial statements is material and pervasive.

Where the auditor concludes that, based on the audit evidence obtained, the financial statements as a whole are not free from material misstatement.

(i) Qualified opinion – where the effect of the subject matter on the financial statements is material but not pervasive

(ii) Disclaimer of opinion – where the effect of the subject matter on the financial statements is material and pervasive.

(**Note**: Full marks will be awarded for describing any two of the above circumstances.)

78 GOING CONCERN

Audit procedures to obtain evidence that the going concern assumption is appropriate are as follows:

- Calculate relevant accounting ratios from the latest available financial statements and consider their trend and significance. For example, the current ratio and quick ratio may warn of declining liquidity. An increasing trade payables period indicates that the entity is struggling to pay its creditors.

- Discuss the matter with the directors. IAS 1 requires the directors to assess the entity's ability to continue as a going concern. The auditors should ask to see this assessment and should decide whether it is convincing.

- Examine budgets or forecast financial statements. If the directors are budgeting to make large profits with significant cash inflows, then going concern is unlikely to be a problem, as long as the budget has been properly prepared. The auditors should assess the assumptions underlying the budget.

- Review correspondence with the bank to assess whether borrowings approaching maturity are likely to be renewed or otherwise re-financed.

- Review correspondence with lawyers to assess whether there are any outstanding claims against the entity that might endanger its future survival if things develop badly.

- Seek written representations from management concerning their view of the future going concern status of the entity and their plans if they foresee serious problems ahead.

79 TOBY

Financial indicators will include:

- An excess of liabilities over assets.
- Net current liabilities.
- Necessary borrowing facilities having not been agreed.

Tutorial note

The requirement here asked for three indicators. Your answer could include points other than those listed above, including the following.

- Default on terms of loan agreements, and potential breaches of covenant.
- Inability to pay debts as they fall due.
- Major losses or cash flow problems, which have arisen since the year-end date and which threaten the company's continued existence.
- Substantial sales of non-current assets not intended to be replaced.
- Denial of (or reduction in) normal terms of trade credit by major suppliers.
- Major debt repayment falling due where refinancing is vital to the company's continued existence.

Non-financial indicators could include:

- Fundamental changes in the environment (e.g. market or technology) to which the company is unable to respond.
- Loss of key management or staff.
- Loss of key suppliers or customers.
- Major litigation in which an adverse judgement may endanger the company's continued existence.
- Major changes in law or other regulations (e.g. pollution control) which may jeopardise the company's operations.

80 GOING CONCERN CONCEPT

(a) The financial statements of an entity should normally be prepared on the presumption that 'the entity will continue in operational existence for the foreseeable future'. This is 12 months from the statement of financial position date. This is the essence of the going concern concept and means specifically that the financial statements of an organisation are prepared on the assumption that there is no intention or necessity to liquidate the organisation or to curtail significantly the scale of its operation.

The major implications of this for the preparation of financial statements include the following:

- assets are recorded and valued on the basis that the organisation expects to recover the recorded amounts in the normal course of business; and
- liabilities are recorded and valued on the basis that they will be paid in the normal course of business.

(b) The going concern concept cannot be used:

- when the company is in liquidation, or
- when the directors see no choice other than to put the company into liquidation.

81 LAMBLEY PROPERTIES

(a) **Explanation to junior auditor**

A written representation letter is an example of 'management' evidence. Management may be tempted to distort the financial statements e.g. to meet the expectations put on a company by shareholders or to hide their own fraudulent activities.

The auditor is unlikely to place the same amount of reliance on management evidence as on either his own or third party evidence because of the inherent bias.

However written evidence is more reliable than oral evidence. In addition, local company law indicates that should management give the auditor knowingly false information, they are guilty of a criminal offence. The auditor can gain some assurance over the quality of evidence because of this provision.

The auditor would be negligent if he relied solely on the written representation letter. The statements in the letter should always be supported by other corroborative evidence.

(b)

Client:	Lambley Properties	W/P Ref:	E1/1
Y/E Date:	31 January 20X3	Prepared by:	RRT
		Date:	2 March 20X3
		Reviewed by:	GL
		Date:	5 March 20X3

Audit Programme: Provision (Legal Claim)

		W/P Ref	Performed by	Reviewed by
1	Examine correspondence with surveyor and lawyer to and from Lambley Properties to obtain relevant information.			
2	Consider reliability of third parties in (1) above.			
3	Consider qualifications and technical ability and experience of third parties in (1) above.			
4	Review other legal correspondence between Lambley Properties and lawyer to obtain information re settlements.			
5	Consider need for independent, third party expert opinion.			

AUDIT REPORT

82 JONES, ROBERTS, WILLIAMS

MEMORANDUM

To: Partners
From: Audit Partner
Date: 30 November 20X8
Re: Audit Problems: Jones, Roberts, Williams, Griffiths

I am currently engaged in reviewing the working papers of several audit assignments which are nearing completion. I have become aware of a number of problem areas in connection with these audits and would value your comments. I have outlined each of the problems below together with the type of qualification in the audit report which I consider may be appropriate in each case.

(a) Jones

The problem and materiality considerations

The amount of the loss at $30,000 represents 20% of pre-tax profit and more than 4% of receivables; it would therefore seem to be material in both profitability and net asset terms, although it is clearly more material in relation to profit.

Relevant accounting principles

The bankruptcy of the debtor indicates that the company has overstated profit and assets as at the year-end by $30,000. This letter provides evidence of a condition existing at the year-end date. This appears to be an adjusting event after the reporting period. It should therefore be treated as an adjusting event.

Form of audit report

The management's refusal to adjust the accounts for the loss means that a disagreement exists between management and the auditor. In such a case, the auditor has to make a decision as to whether the amount of the loss is 'pervasive' or 'material but not pervasive' or, possibly (but unlikely here), not even material. Without more facts being available, it is difficult to draw conclusions satisfactorily in this area, but on the face of it a qualified *except for" form of audit qualification would appear appropriate as the true and fair view would not be entirely destroyed if the loss were to remain unadjusted.

(b) Roberts

The problem and materiality considerations

The amount of $10,000 represents only 2% of the stated profit before tax of $500,000 and does not, in itself, appear to be material in terms of its impact on the financial statements. Unfortunately, however, the potential losses may be very much more significant than the figure of $10,000, since other claims are now pending, and the auditor may have to conclude that the whole legal matter is potentially material.

Relevant accounting principles

It seems likely that a liability to transfer economic benefits exists here, which can be measured with a reasonable degree of reliability, and, as such, a provision should be recorded as a liability in the financial statements.

Form of audit report

There is clearly uncertainty with regard to the outcome of the pending claims and the potential liability which they represent. The auditor will have to decide whether or not the possibility of loss is likely or remote. Management has apparently chosen to ignore both the actual loss (which is not of itself material) and the potential loss (which may well be material). If the auditor can be convinced that management's view is acceptable and the disclosure in the notes is adequate, then a qualification may be avoidable. The auditor should be aware, however, that items which are not material when considered individually may well have a cumulative effect which is material in total. If the auditor does not believe that the management's view is acceptable, or does not think that the disclosure is adequate, then there is a disagreement as to the way in which the uncertainty has been treated. In this case, a 'qualified' opinion is probably sufficient. However, if the auditor believes that the claims are likely to be successful and are likely to be substantial then it may be necessary to issue an adverse opinion.

(c) **Williams**

The problem and materiality considerations

The loans are not irrecoverable debts and so have no effect on the reported loss. However, this sort of matter cannot have the same materiality test applied to it as in the cases relating to the clients dealt with above. Amounts owed by directors are required to be disclosed as a requirement of company law. Materiality should, therefore, not be measured in relation to profit or loss for the year or the net assets position, but in relation to the requirements of the law. It would appear that the loans are not allowed and that Williams is materially in non-compliance with company law.

Relevant accounting principles

As mentioned in the question, the loans are not allowed and disclosure should in any case be made. The item should be separately disclosed and cannot be 'hidden' as part of a figure containing other 'receivables collectable within one year'.

Form of audit report

The standard audit report in many countries requires the auditor to state specifically whether or not the financial statements comply with relevant company law. The financial statements of Williams do not fully comply with such requirements. The fact that Williams is a manufacturing business would indicate that such loans to directors would not be made in the normal course of business, as could be argued if the company were a bank, for example. In these circumstances, the auditor is required to include details of the loans in the audit report, and to qualify the report by stating that the loans contravene the provisions of the relevant statute. Even though the loans were subsequently repaid there may still be a requirement to disclose the amounts outstanding during the year and the auditor will need to confirm this by reviewing the country's legislation and IAS® Standards being used.

83 TAGGART

(a)

Accountants & Co
Lowton

The Directors
Taggart
Lowton

12 January 20X8

Dear Sirs,

Accounting treatment of sale with option to buy back

This transaction has given Taggart some cash now, in return for a repayment with interest in four years' time. The auditor will require sight of the 'sale' document, and will discuss the matter with the directors to try and determine the exact nature of the transaction.

There are two alternatives here; either the transaction is bona fide, in which case no further action is required; or the transaction is an attempt to give finance to the company in the form of a loan which will not be shown on the statement of financial position. If the latter situation is true, then Taggart is involved in an 'unrecognised financing' arrangement, i.e. obtaining a loan which will not be shown in the statement of financial position. The auditor would require that the commercial substance of the transaction be shown in the financial statements, and not the legal form of the transaction. In this way the financial statements will show a true and fair view.

To show the commercial substance of the transaction it will be necessary to show the amount of money received as a loan in the financial statements. The 'sale' will similarly be cancelled and the brandy placed back into inventory. The interest on the loan will be calculated annually and added to the amount of the loan, having been charged against profits. In this way the loan will be repaid without loss when it comes to term.

If Taggart did not accept this method of disclosing this 'quasi loan' then an audit modification would be required – a 'qualified opinion'.

If you have any further questions regarding this matter please do not hesitate to contact me.

Yours faithfully,

ANSWERS TO PRACTICE QUESTIONS : SECTION 4

(b)
                                                                                  Accountants & Co
                                                                                                                                 Lowton

The Directors
Wolfworld
Lowton

12 January 20X8

Dear Sirs,

Accounting treatment of revaluations

The revaluations carried out by Wolfworld are acceptable, as is the method of calculating the amount of the depreciation charge. The directors then want to continue charging the historical cost part of the depreciation against realised profits, but charge that part of depreciation relating to the revalued amount against the revaluation reserve. This will have the effect of splitting the depreciation charge. The directors' logic here is that their disclosed expense for depreciation will still be comparable with companies who have not revalued their non-current assets.

Standard accounting practice requires that all depreciation be charged against profits. There should be a consistency of accounting treatment between the statement of financial position and what is charged against realised profits in the statement of comprehensive income. The actions of the directors of Wolfworld are therefore in conflict with generally accepted accounting principles.

We recommend that you amend your depreciation treatment. If this is not done then an 'qualified opinion' may be necessary in the audit report as a consequence of the above disagreement concerning the accounting treatment.

If you have any further queries regarding this matter please do not hesitate to contact me.

Yours faithfully,

84   B CO

There is no clear definition of truth and fairness, even though this concept lies at the very heart of financial reporting and audit. The auditors must consider a host of factors in deciding whether the accounts give a true and fair view.

The auditors will review the accounting policies that we adopt in the preparation of our financial statements. These must comply with the accounting standards published by the accountancy profession and with company law. They must also be consistent with those applied by us in previous years.

The auditors will also consider the factual accuracy of the information published in the statements. They will devote a great deal of care and attention to the detailed testing of the accounting records and will post these balances through to the final accounts.

The statements must also provide sufficient disclosure to enable a reader to form an adequate understanding of our financial position and performance. At the very least, they will have to meet the minimum requirements laid down by law and by professional standards, but it may be necessary for them to go beyond this in order to give a true and fair view.

Any failure to meet the above requirements will have to be reviewed for materiality. The auditors might disagree with us for some reason, but could still conclude that the accounts give a true and fair view because their reservations would not affect the behaviour of a reader of the accounts.

85 GEE

A qualified opinion means any situation where the auditor cannot report without reservation that the financial statements show a true and fair view. This means that the opinion paragraph will be modified to include the qualification and an additional paragraph added to the audit report to explain the basis or reason for the qualification.

The auditor should express a qualified opinion where either:

- the auditor, having obtained sufficient appropriate audit evidence concludes that misstatements, individually or in aggregate are material but not pervasive to the financial statements, or
- the auditor is unable to obtain sufficient appropriate audit evidence on which to base the opinion, but the auditor concludes that the possible effects on the financial statements, if any, could be material but not pervasive *Modifications to the opinion in the independent auditor's report* (ISA 705).

86 BUTCAR AND COMPANY

(a) An audit firm should express an unmodified opinion in its report on the financial statements of a company when the auditor believes, from his work and tests performed, that the financial statements do reflect a true and fair view and have been correctly prepared.

(b) (i) **Analytical procedures are used to compare relationships between different variables.** For example, an auditor could calculate financial ratios and compare them with last year's ratios calculated for the clients' competitors or industry standard ratios. By undertaking comparisons the auditor will identify any unusual trends or fluctuations and investigate them.

In addition, an auditor could examine clients financial forecasts e.g. profit forecast or cash flow forecast and compare them to last year, competitors or industry standards. Again any unusual fluctuations or regular patterns will be highlighted.

(ii) **Analytical procedures at the planning stage:**

Butcar & Company (the auditors) should use analytical procedures at the planning stage of the audit to identify the potential high risk areas of the audit of Colain. In addition the procedures would also enable the auditors to assist in their understanding of the business of their client and to facilitate the planning of audit tests to be carried out.

Using analytical procedures at the planning stage will assist the auditors in identifying issues that they may not be aware of, for example by comparing non-current asset totals in the statement of financial position will alert the auditors that Colain may have acquired non-current assets during the year. This will enable the auditors to design audit procedures to ensure that the non-current asset additions are treated correctly in the financial statements i.e. proper disclosure and valuation.

Other examples of using analytical procedures at the planning stage include:

- Calculating and comparing gross profit margins with the current financial year and the previous financial year will highlight a possible increase or decrease in sales and/or an increase or decrease in cost of sales. This could indicate overtrading for example.
- Calculating and comparing the receivables collection days will identify if it is taking longer for Colain to collect its debts from trade customers. These ratios could also indicate potential cash flow problems if it is taking longer to collect its debts.

Once the auditors have calculated some ratios and made comparisons with last year, they could then identify relationships in the ratios they have calculated. For example an increase in receivable days and a corresponding increase in sales would indicate that more sales have been made on credit, possibly to new trade customers. This could result in the need for an increase in doubtful debt provision.

The analytical procedures used by the auditors at the planning stage will enable them to allocate resources to the more 'high risk' aspects of the audit and enable the auditors to plan the overall audit more effectively.

Analytical procedures at the final overall review stage

Once the audit work has been completed the review stage will ensure that sufficient, relevant and reliable evidence has been gathered and that the evidence gathered supports the conclusion reached i.e. that the financial statements do or do not represent a true and fair view.

Analytical review procedures at this stage will help the auditors to identify if they have gathered sufficient, relevant and reliable evidence. For example, if the auditors identified that Colain had acquired additional non-current assets by analytical procedures then the auditors would have ensured that the effects of the acquisitions were fully reflected in the financial statements of Colain.

The auditors will also be able to use analytical procedures to make an assessment of the reasonableness of the overall financial statements when compared with the sector specific industry average. For example, a fall in sales as reported in the financial statements of Colain can be compared with the average sales of a similar company in the textile manufacturing industry. This would be a good indicator as to the current situation in the textile sector as a fall in sales reported by Colain and the sector as a whole could indicate potential future problems for Colain.

In addition the auditors could assess whether the evidence that they have gathered is consistent with the analytical procedures carried out during the final review stage of the audit. For example, an increase in inventory levels and a corresponding decrease in sales should be supported by directors' explanations as to why sales have fallen plus detailed inventory records of inventory levels rising. A comparison with the sector as a whole should again be made to confirm whether audit evidence is consistent with analytical procedures carried out by the auditors.

87 TYPES OF AUDIT OPINION

(i) Disclaimer of opinion:

The auditor shall disclaim an opinion when the auditor is unable to obtain sufficient appropriate audit evidence on which to base the opinion and the auditor concludes that the possible effects on the financial statements of undetected misstatements, if any could be both material and pervasive.

(ii) Adverse opinion:

The auditor, having obtained sufficient, appropriate audit evidence, concludes that misstatements, individually or in the aggregate, are both material and pervasive to the financial statements *Modifications to the opinion in the independent auditor's report*. (ISA 705).

Section 5

JUNE 2012 EXAM QUESTIONS

SECTION A – ALL TEN QUESTIONS ARE COMPULSORY AND MUST BE ATTEMPTED

1   All students of ACCA are bound by its *'Code of Ethics and Conduct'*.

   Is this statement true or false?

   A   True

   B   False   (1 mark)

2   Which of the following should be held on a trade receivables master file?

   (1)   Customer credit limits

   (2)   Customer reference numbers

   (3)   Cumulative sales data

   A   (1) only

   B   (2) only

   C   (3) only

   D   (1) and (2)   (2 marks)

3   Which of the following statements is FALSE with regard to audit planning?

   A   It helps the auditors to devote appropriate attention to important areas of the financial statements.

   B   It helps the auditor to properly organize and manage the audit engagement, so that it is performed in an effective manner.

   C   It provides assurance to the auditor that the risk of a material misstatement in the financial statements will be reduced.

   D   It facilitates the direction and supervision of audit team members and the review of their work.   (3 marks)

4   'The materiality level calculated at the planning stage should NOT be revised during later stages of the audit'.

   Is this statement true or false?

   A   True

   B   False   (1 mark)

FAU: FOUNDATIONS IN AUDIT

5   In which of the following audit situations should an auditor maintain professional scepticism?

(1) When reviewing the results of a trade receivables circularisation

(2) When considering verbal representations made by the directors of the company

(3) When considering written representations made by the directors of the company

(4) When cross-checking a bank reconciliation prepared by the cashier of the company

A   (1) and (4) only

B   (2) and (3) only

C   (2), (3) and (4) only

D   (1), (2) (3) and (4) (3 marks)

6   Which of the following factors could be the reason for an INCREASE in reported gross profit in the financial statements of a company?

(1) A reduction in carriage outward costs for the period under review

(2) A reduction in carriage inwards costs for the period under review

(3) An increase in the amount of discount received from suppliers of components for early payment of purchases invoices

A   (1) and (2) only

B   (2) only

C   (3) only

D   (1), (2) and (3) (2 marks)

7   'The authority of international standards on Auditing always overrides national regulations governing the audit of the financial statements of companies in a given country.'

Is this statement true or false?

A   True

B   False (1 mark)

8   Which of the following factors should have the effect of INCREASING a sample size for a test of details?

(1) An increase in the use of other substantive procedures directed at the same assertion

(2) An increase in the amount of misstatement that the auditor expects to find in the population

(3) An increase in the level of tolerable misstatement

A   (1) only

B   (2) only

C   (2) and (3)

D   (3) only (2 marks)

JUNE 12 EXAM QUESTIONS : **SECTION 5**

9   Which of the following financial statement assertions should an auditor use when checking 'account balances at the period end' in a set of financial statements?

   A   Accuracy

   B   Cut-off

   C   Existence

   D   Occurrence (3 marks)

10 Which of the following descriptors are assumed to apply to a set of financial statements on which an auditor has expressed an unmodified opinion?

   (1) They adequately disclose the significant accounting policies selected and applied.

   (2) They reflect all transactions entered into by the company for the period under review.

   (3) They disclose information which is complete and totally accurate in every respect, except for accounting for estimated which by their very nature cannot be totally correct.

   A   (1) only

   B   (1) and (2)

   C   (2) only

   D   (3) only (2 marks)

   (Total: 20 marks)

FAU: FOUNDATIONS IN AUDIT

SECTION B – ALL NINE QUESTIONS ARE COMPULSORY AND MUST BE ATTEMPTED

1 INTERNAL CONTROL

At a recent audit seminar, the speaker emphasized the importance of good internal control in audit client companies. He explained the components of internal control but stressed that there are inherent limitations to any internal control system.

Required:

(a) Explain the purpose if 'internal control'. (4 marks)

(b) Identify THREE components of the internal control of a company. (6 marks)

(c) Identify ONE inherent limitation of any internal control system and for the limitation identified, provide an example of it. (5 marks)

(Total: 15 marks)

2 RIVER CO

River Co manufactures office furniture and has been an audit client of your firm for many years. Your firm is planning the audit of the company's financial statements for the year ending 31 July 20X2.

In a recent email to the audit engagement partner, the company's managing director stated that, unfortunately, the company would not be able to provide staff to supervise the year-end inventory count, due to a shortage of available staff with appropriate experience. Given its knowledge of the company, he therefore requested that your firm provide staff to supervise the count. He has offered to pay your firm a premium rate fee for the supervision of the count and considers that it would be money well spent as, in his view, it would mean that the directors of River Co would not be responsible for the accuracy of the inventory count as a basis for the value of inventory to be reported in the company's financial statements.

Required:

(a) (i) State the purpose of an auditor's attendance at a client's year-end inventory count. (4 marks)

    (ii) Explain how your firm's audit engagement partner should respond to the request from River Co's managing director, to supervise the year-end inventory count. (5 marks)

(b) Identify TWO audit procedures with regard to inventory that members of your firm's audit team should carry out AFTER attending the year-end inventory count. (6 marks)

(Total: 15 marks)

JUNE 12 EXAM QUESTIONS : SECTION 5

3 LAKE CO

The directors of Lake Co recently discovered a wages fraud at the company, so they are now seeking advice on the design and implementation of a new wages system which will incorporate appropriate segregation of duties.

Required:

(a) State TWO objectives of the internal control that should be exercised over the wages system of Lake Co. (4 marks)

(b) Explain the meaning of 'segregation of duties'. (3 marks)

(c) Identify the THREE aspects pertaining to wages transactions that should be subject to segregation of duties (3 marks)

(Total: 10 marks)

4 GOING CONCERN

Management should consider a range of issues and information concerning the company's future performance when assessing their company's ability to continue as a going concern, for example the identification of future risks and uncertainties that could affect that ability.

Required:

(a) Explain what is meant by the 'going concern assumption'. (4 marks)

(b) Identify and explain TWO matters of pieces of information that an auditor should consider when evaluating management's assessment of their company's ability to continue as a going concern. (6 marks)

(Total: 10 marks)

5 DIRECTION AND SUPERVISION

Required:

Identify and explain TWO factors that determine the nature, timing and extent of the direction and supervision of audit engagement team members and the review of their work. (6 marks)

6 FLOWCHARTS

Required:

State TWO advantages and ONE disadvantage of auditors using flowcharts to record information systems and internal control. (6 marks)

7 DEFINITIONS

Required:

Define the following:

(a) A substantive procedure (3 marks)

(b) A test of control (3 marks)

(Total: 6 marks)

KAPLAN PUBLISHING

8 CIRCULARISATION OF RECEIVABLES

David commenced trading as a sole trader on 1 October 20X1. David decided to prepare accounts to 30 April each year.

Required:

With regard to a circularisation of trade receivables:

(a) Explain what is meant by:

    (i) A positive circularisation   (2 marks)

    (ii) A negative circularisation   (2 marks)

(b) Identify TWO classes of trade receivable account that would require special attention for inclusion in a circularisation. (2 marks)

(Total: 6 marks)

9 AUDIT OF ACCRUALS

Required:

Explain two procedures that should be used to audit accruals.

(Total: 6 marks)

Section 6

ANSWERS TO JUNE 2012 EXAM QUESTIONS

SECTION A

1 A

All ACCA members, including student members, are bound by ACCA's *Code of Ethics and Conduct*.

2 D

Customer credit limits and customer reference numbers should be held on a trade receivables master file. Cumulative sales data should be held on data files.

3 C

Audit planning benefits the audit of financial statements in various ways. Three of which are listed as items A, B and D. Adequate audit planning would not provide any assurance concerning the risk of the existence of material misstatement in a set of financial statements.

4 B

The statement is false. The materiality level calculated when planning the audit may need to be revised as the audit progresses. For example, then it appears that the actual financial results for the period are significantly different from those that were used in calculating the materiality level at the planning stage.

5 D

An auditor should maintain professional scepticism throughout an audit engagement.

6 B

Efficiency savings made as a consequence of early payment discount received from suppliers should not be reflected in the trading account part of the statement of profit or loss. Consequently, such savings would have no effect on reported gross profit. Carriage outwards costs should similarly not be charged in the trading account: therefore a reduction in these will have no effect on gross profit. As carriage inward costs are part of cost of dales, any reduction in them could account for an increase in gross profit.

KAPLAN PUBLISHING

7   B

The authority of International Standards on Auditing (ISAs) is secondary to national regulations governing the audit of financial statements.

8   B

Of the factors stated, only that at (2) – an increase in the amount of misstatement the auditor expects to find in the population – should have the effect of increasing the sample size for a test of details.

9   C

ISA 315 *Identifying and Assessing the Risks of Material Misstatement through Understanding the Entity and its Environment* provides examples of the assertions used by auditors when testing assertions about account balances at the period end. Of the assertions listed only that of 'existence' should be used.

10   A

Due to the concept of 'reasonable assurance' it should not be assumed that such financial statements reflect all transactions entered into by the company for the period under review (option C). Similarly it should not be assumed that the information disclosed in such financial statements is totally correct.

SECTION B

1   INTERNAL CONTROL

Key answer tips

Question 1 will be worth 15 marks and will be on any topic. It may be split into more than one question requirement.

(a)   ISA 315 *Identifying and Assessing the Risks of Material Misstatement through Understanding the Entity and its Environment* explains that the purpose of internal control is to address identified business risks that concern:

   1   The reliability of the entity's financial reporting.

   2   The effectiveness and efficiency of its operations.

   3   The compliance with laws and regulations.

   (Full marks will be awarded for answers presenting the points as above or in similar fashion.)

(b) The five components of a company's internal control system are:

1. The control environment.

2. The company's risk assessment process.

3. The information system, including the related business processes, relevant to financial reporting, and communication.

4. Control activities relevant to the audit, and

5. Monitoring of controls.

(Full marks will be awarded for identifying THREE of the above components.)

(c) Inherent limitations of any internal control system and examples of each include:

1. Human judgement – faulty decision-making or human error may lead to breakdowns in internal control. For example, in the design of computer processing controls.

2. Failure to understand or take action – there may be ineffective control because individuals may not understand the purpose of a specific control. For example, the purpose of a payroll exception report.

3. Inappropriate management override of controls – management may purposefully override existing controls, thus rendering laid down system controls to be ineffective. For example, a sales director may choose to opt to extend credit to a long-standing customer in order to create customer goodwill, in contravention of laid down credit control procedures.

4. Collusion by two or more people – leading to circumnavigation of controls. For example, between a factory employee, factory manager and a wages data processing clerk to claim, authorise and process a fraudulent payment for overtime wages.

5. Management judgement – with regard to the nature and extent of risk the company chooses to assume and the nature and extent of the controls it chooses to implement. For example, management may adopt a low risk exposure to the loss of non-current assets by implementing an ongoing system of monitoring and inspection of non-current assets, centred around the operation of a comprehensively detailed non-current asset register.

6. Cost benefit consideration – a pragmatic approach will often need to be adopted in this regard, especially in smaller companies. For example, the cost of employing additional accounts staff to ensure adequate segregation of duties in relevant areas may outweigh the maximum benefit to be derived from improved internal control.

7. Ability to cope with non-routine transactions – the ability to predict the likelihood of non-routine transactions arising means that it is less likely that systems will be designed to cope with such transactions. For example, the purchase of a very expensive non-current asset with an unusual and complex specification.

(Full marks will be awarded for identifying and providing an example of any ONE of the above limitations and for providing an appropriate example of it.)

2 RIVER CO

Key answer tips

Question 2 will be worth 15 marks and will be on any topic. It will frequently be split into more than one question requirement.

(a) (i) The purpose of an auditor's attendance at a client's year-end inventory count is to assess the effectiveness of the client's inventory counting procedures in order to determine whether reliance can be placed upon them to provide assurance about the existence and condition of inventory.

(ii) My firm's audit engagement partner should respond by politely explaining that he would not be able to provide audit staff to supervise the year-end inventory count of River Co. His explanation should refer to the fact that the responsibility for the contents, the truth and fairness and the preparation of the company's annual financial statements lies solely with the company's directors, and that this cannot be delegated. Similarly he should confirm that it is my firm's duty, as the company's auditors, to prepare an auditor's report addressed to the shareholders of the company, about the truth and fairness of the financial statements. There is an underlying presumption that the firm will be objective when preparing the report and there would be a self-review threat to objectivity if employees or partners of it had an active involvement in the inventory count.

(b) Members of my firm's audit team should carry out the following procedures after the year-end inventory count:

- Check to ensure that all sheets and records used at the inventory count are included in the final inventory count sheets and records.
- Trace items that were test counted at the inventory count to ensure correct quantities are included in the sheets and records to be used in the valuation process.
- Ensure that slow-moving and obsolete inventory lines recorded at the inventory count are properly highlighted in the sheets and records to be used in the valuation process.
- Confirm that the current cut-off procedures have been properly applied by checking a sample of goods received notes and goods despatched notes. These should represent receipts and despatches both immediately before and immediately after the year-end date.
- Confirm the cost calculations applied to both inventory and work-in-progress. This will involve checking back to costing records, purchase invoices and wages costs as appropriate. Special attention will need to be paid to the inclusion of overheads in work-in-progress and finished goods inventory.
- Confirm the net realisable value of inventory by checking forward to sales of inventory sold after the date of the statement of financial position. Compare this to cost values as determined (above) and ensure inventory is valued at lower of the two.
- Carry out analytical review procedures on inventory to obtain assurance about the completeness, accuracy and valuation assertions.

- Ensure the adequacy of the presentation of the disclosure of inventory by checking to the underlying accounting records.
- Check replies from third parties about inventory held by or for them.

(Full marks will be awarded for answers which include TWO of the above or other relevant procedures.)

3 LAKE CO

Key answer tips

Question 3 will be worth 10 marks and will be on any topic. Some of the 10-mark requirements may be split into more than one requirement.

(a) The objectives of the internal control that should be exercised over the wages system of Lake Co include:

(i) To ensure that all work paid for is for the benefit of the company.

(ii) To ensure that all authorised work and only authorised work is paid for.

(iii) To ensure that wages are currently calculated.

(iv) To ensure that wages are paid only to authorised employees of the company.

(v) To ensure that timely payment is made to employees of the company for work carried out.

(vi) To ensure that wages deductions are correctly calculated.

(vii) To ensure that wages deductions are paid on a timely basis to relevant authorities.

(viii) To ensure that all wages transactions are completed and accurately recorded in the company's accounting records on a timely basis.

(Full marks will be awarded for stating TWO of the above or other appropriate objectives.)

(b) 'Segregation of duties' is used to describe the condition which should exist in the internal control exercised over any functional area, whereby no individual person is responsible for more than one of the following duties:

(i) the authorisation of a transaction;

(ii) the recording of the transaction in the accounting records; and

(iii) the custody of the asset relating to the transaction.

(Full marks will be awarded for the identification of (i), (ii) and (iii) above.)

(c) The three aspects pertaining to wages that should be subject to segregation of duties are:

(i) Authorisation of wages payable to employees.

(ii) Processing/recording of wages in the accounting records.

(iii) Payment of wages to employees.

4 GOING CONCERN

Key answer tips

Question 4 will be worth 10 marks and will be on any topic. Where the requirement is split into more than one requirement, they will often be on related issues.

(a) Under the 'going concern assumption', an entity is ordinarily viewed as continuing in business for the foreseeable future, to a date at least, but not limited to, 12 months form the end of the reporting period., with neither the necessity of liquidation, cessation, of trading or the seeking of protection from creditors pursuant to laws. Accordingly assets and liabilities are recorded on the basis that the entity will be able to realise its assets and liabilities in the normal course of business.

(Full marks will be awarded for answers containing the points included as above.)

(b) Auditors should consider the following matters and pieces of information when evaluating management's assessment of their company's ability to continue as a going concern:

1. The period used by management in assessing going concern. This should be at least 12 months from the date of the financial statements.

2. The systems used for the identification of future risks and uncertainties. This will vary between sectors and companies – but may, for example, include market research systems, expert analysis or computer modelling techniques.

3. Budget and forecast information including the quality of systems used to produce this information.

4. Underlying assumptions made with regard to budgets and forecast information. Owing to the nature of these assumptions it is particularly important that the auditor should maintain a degree of professional scepticism when considering the assumptions. Attention should be given to the accuracy of assumptions underlying earlier budgets and forecasts made by management.

5. The sensitivity of budgets and forecasts – the auditor should carry out a sensitivity analysis of the company's budget and forecasts to possible changing circumstances, if this has not already been carried out by the company.

6. The existence of any obligations/undertakings or guarantees arranged with lenders and suppliers. The possible effect of these on future operations of the company is a vital consideration.

7. The availability of borrowing facilities to the company and the likelihood of these being withdrawn in the foreseeable future. These could be crucial to the company's ongoing existence as a going concern and need to be carefully reviewed.

8. Management's plans for future actions – these will vary dependent on circumstances but the auditor should, where appropriate, consider previous undertakings by management to carry out specified actions and the subsequent success of these in achieving desired objectives.

(Full marks will be awarded for answers identifying and explaining TWO of the above matters.)

5 DIRECTION AND SUPERVISION

Key answer tips

Question 5 will be worth 6 marks and will be on any topic. In this exam, it is a single requirement, although it could be split into several requirements.

Factors that determine the nature, timing and extent of the direction and supervision of audit engagement team members and the review of their work include:

- The capabilities and competence of the individual team members performing the audit work. Less experienced and less qualified members will, for example, require closer monitoring and supervision than more experienced and better qualified members.

- The size and complexity of the company. For example, the direction and supervision and review of work of members of a large team engaged on the audit of the financial statements of a national multi-site company would present a completely different challenge to similar tasks pertaining to a small single-site locally based company.

- The area of the financial statements being audited. In a car manufacturing company, for example, the work of team members engaged in the audit of the reported inventory balance (including work-in-progress) would probably require closer direction, supervision and review than the work of others engaged in the audit of the reported bank balance.

- The assessed risks of material misstatement. For example, where for a given area of an audit there is increased inherent risk and control risk, ordinarily there will need to be an increased level of direction and supervision of engagement team members and review of their work.

(Full marks will be awarded for answers identifying and explaining TWO of the above or other relevant factors.)

6 FLOWCHARTS

Key answer tips

Question 6 will be worth 6 marks and will be on any topic. In this case, there is one single requirement to deal with.

Flowcharts – advantages	Flowcharts – disadvantages
• Information is presented in a logical sequence	• Not generally suitable for recording systems with numerous unusual transactions
• They ensure that a system is recorded in its entirety as all documents have to be traced from beginning to end.	• Only suitable for describing standard systems
• Facilitates easy understanding of a system	• Major amendment is not normally possible without redrawing
• Serves as a permanent record of a system that can be subject to a minor amendment on a year-to-year basis	• Time can be wasted by recording and checking areas that are of no audit significance
• They can be prepared quickly by staff with little experience	• They are not normally appropriate for recording systems where there are subsystems or subroutines

7 DEFINITIONS

Key answer tips

Question 7 will be worth 6 marks and will be on any topic. In this case, there are two requirements which carry an equal number of marks. You should therefore ensure that you spent an equal amount of time answering each part of the question.

(a) A substantive procedure is designed to detect material misstatements at the assertion level. Substantive procedures comprise:

(i) Tests of details (of classes of transactions, account balances and disclosures) and

(ii) Substantive analytical procedures.

(b) A test of control is an audit procedure designed to evaluate the operating effectiveness of controls in preventing or detecting and correcting material misstatements at the assertion level.

(Full marks will be awarded for definitions which are similar to the above.)

8 CIRCULARISATION OF RECEIVABLES

Key answer tips

Question 8 will be 6 marks and on any topic.

(a) (i) A positive circularisation consists of letters sent to a sample of trade receivable customers who are asked to confirm, directly to the auditor, the accuracy (or otherwise) of the stated balance as shown in the audit client company's trade receivables ledger for the subject customer. Where customers disagree with the stated balance they are asked to state the nature of their disagreement.

(ii) A negative circularisation consists of letters sent to a sample of trade receivables customers, who are asked to respond directly to the auditor, only if they disagree with the stated balance as shown in the audit client's trade receivables ledger for the subject customer.

(b) The following classes of account would require special attention for inclusion in the circularisation:

- Dormant accounts.
- Accounts with material balances.
- Accounts with nil balances.
- Accounts with credit balances.
- Accounts with long outstanding balances.
- Accounts on which there have been contras with trade payables account balances.
- Accounts containing a significant number of journal adjustments.
- Accounts settled by round sum amounts.
- Accounts containing unusual transactions.
- Accounts to which credit notes or journals have been posted close to the period end.
- Accounts written-off during the period under review.
- Accounts which have been paid by the date of the circularisation.

(Full marks will be awarded for stating any TWO of the above or other relevant classes of account.)

9 AUDIT OF ACCRUALS

Key answer tips

Question 9 will be 6 marks and on any topic.

The following procedures should be carried out to audit accruals:

- Compare the list of accruals to those for the previous period to obtain assurance as to the completeness of the accruals.
- Review expense categories included in the income statement to identify areas of possible accruals and check to list of accruals for inclusion.
- Sample check computations of accruals by comparing to earlier relevant invoices and payment records.
- Scrutinise payments made after the date of the statement of financial position to identify accruals possibly omitted and to check accuracy of calculated accruals.
- Consider the basis for and accuracy of round sum accrual amounts.
- Check for the existence of wages accruals and compute to ensure the completeness and accuracy of these.
- Check for the existence of a sales tax account and compute to ensure the completeness and accuracy of this. Agree the last amount paid in the accounting period per the cash book to the return. Tests should include checking reasonableness of final return in period to following return where appropriate.
- Test transactions around the accounting period end to determine whether amounts have been recognised in the correct period.

(**Note:** Full marks will be awarded for explaining TWO of the above or other relevant procedures.)